AN ILLUSTRATED HISTORY

AN ILLUSTRATED HISTORY

SHAUN BARRINGTON

This edition published by
Barnes & Noble, Inc.,
by arrangement with
PRC Publishing Ltd.

Produced by
PRC Publishing Ltd
64 Brewery Road
London N7 9NT
A member of the Chrysalis
Group plc

ISBN 1-56619-466-0

Printed in China

Reprinted 1995, 1996, 1997,
1998, 2001, 2002

PAGE 1: A 1992 Heritage Softail.

PAGES 2-3: Gleaming bikes with Evo engines in the Utah desert.

RIGHT: The 1200 cc XCH Sportster – the big one – on Capitol Drive where they make the heart of the beast.

DSON

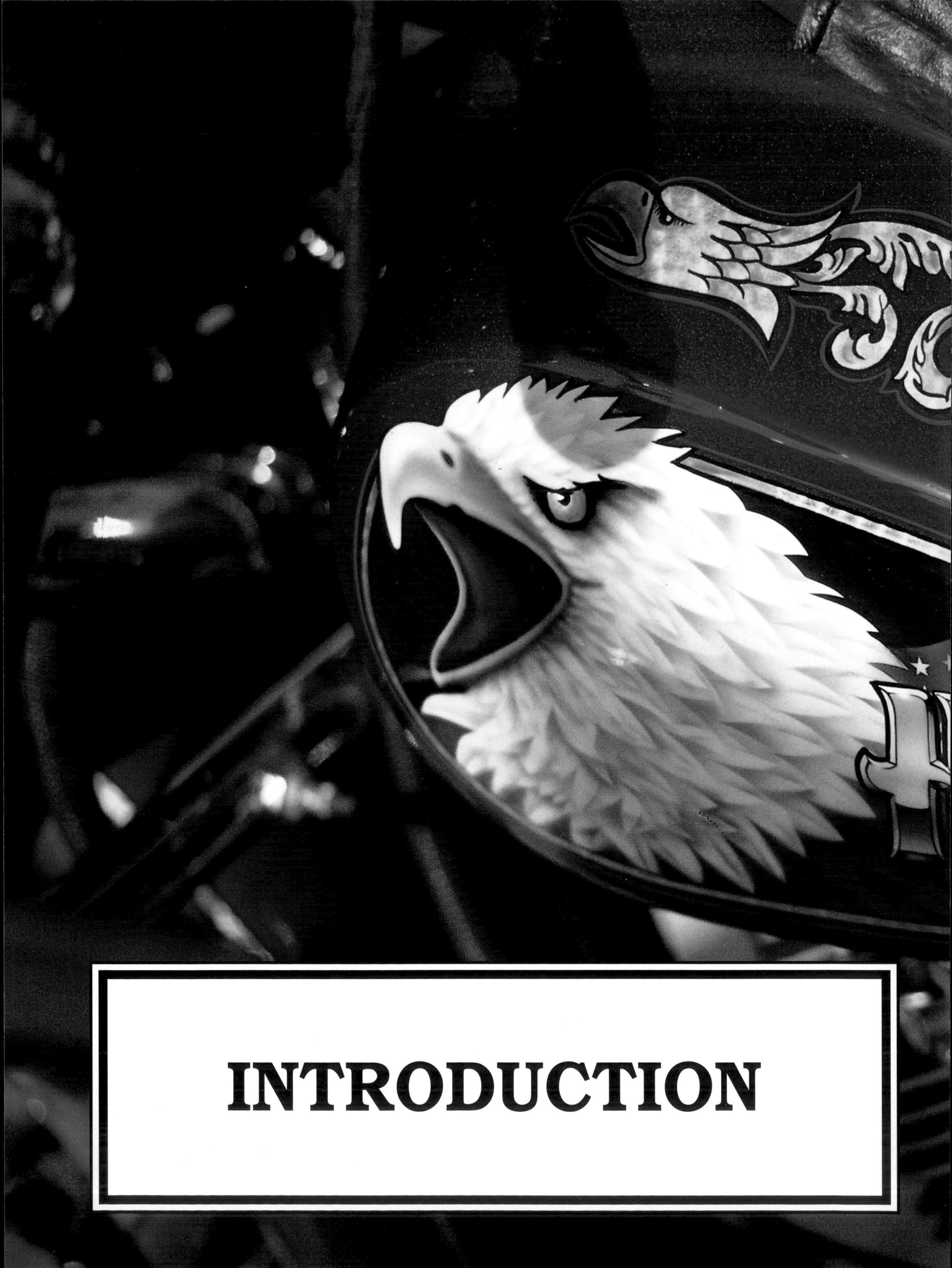

INTRODUCTION

RIGHT: The sheer number of contemporary Harley-Davidsons is proof in itself of the conservative/nostalgic ethos of the company. The fender and forks of this Special Edition Electra Glide could be straight from the 1950s. With over 90 years in business, there have been lots of excuses for anniversary limited editions and Harley-Davidson have produced several over the last two decades.

PREVIOUS PAGES: The screaming eagle and the Stars and Stripes; it didn't take long for the fledgling company to understand that their machines could be sold as a uniquely American institution, and beautiful individual paintwork like this reinforces the patriotic association today.

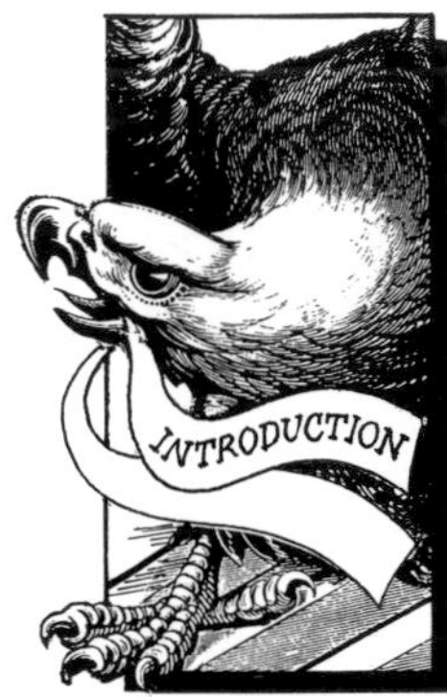

In 1903, Bill Harley and Arthur, Walter and Bill Davidson rolled their first production motorcycle out the door of their 10 by 15 foot 'factory' . . . Well, of course the best way to tell a story like this is to start at the beginning and, fortunately for those who have a feeling not just for motorcycles, but for endeavor and creativity wherever it shines, we can't just go on until we get to the end. There *is* no end to the Milwaukee story. But a few observations can be forgiven before the story proper concerning the word "image."

So we'll start, a little unconventionally perhaps, with an advertisement for Jeeps. The advert mentions Zippo lighters and blue jeans – American icons to be venerated and associated with that revamped warhorse – and you can almost imagine the beleaguered copywriter being beaten with his own red suspenders for adding "Harley-Davidson", a rival ousted in the Second World War when it came to traversing the swamps of the Pacific, but not always beaten in the showroom. Jeans, Jeeps, Zippos, Harleys – lifestyle accessories of the American Way, images to be exploited by the Madison Avenue cultural pirates. But there is one essential fact about these icons, these images, that is easily forgotten. They are *functional*, they *work*, and they have proved their durability and usefulness over time. You can't chop an image, you can't make a dragster out of an icon, you can't decide in August to run a symbol across to Sturgis to check out all the other symbols. A Harley-Davidson, be it a Sportster, a Tourer or an Aermacchi, by and large does what it is supposed to do. Incidentally, it looks right when it's doing it.

If the overall performance (and no, that doesn't mean top speed) of, say, a Honda GoldWing, was so much better than an Electra Glide, of course many riders would still grumble into their beards about Japanese toys and stick with the home-grown machine. (Journalist Hugo Wilson caught the mood perfectly by suggesting that the designers of the Honda "had obviously been keeping an eye on recent developments in bathroom fittings," (*What Bike*, November 1993). But eventually the xenophobia would be worn down and the market would be lost to the eastern invaders. Indeed, hundreds of thousands have bought the GoldWing, and the US is far and away its most important market. Technologically, the original flat four, water-cooled, belt-driven dohc 999 cc machine (soon upsized to 1100, 1200 and later six cylinder 1500) appeared to be ahead of the game and Honda (incorrectly) claimed to have produced the first motorcycle with water cooling. But the machine was introduced practically in the Dark Ages – 1975 – and you still see the odd Harley on the road. Honda should have won the battle by now. I do not believe that this survival is solely dependent upon mere sentiment. It has as much to do with riding position and reliability.

A Harley-Davidson does provide mileage

Special Edition Electra-Glide

RIGHT: **An image that is immediately recognizable the world over, one which cries "freedom." In the foreground, a Softail Custom, behind it an earlier Shovelhead. Not surprisingly, the American southwest has always been the major market for such machinery, where the weather is kind and invites you to saddle up and go.**

for the poseur, of course, but ego gratification is a relative thing. In comparison with a Jaguar XJ220 or a McLaren F1, a top-of-the-range Bimota, even a sports truck, it is of course too cheap to be a simple status symbol (though don't say that to us ordinary mortals trying to upgrade to a Glide). Harley owners are not sentimentalists and nor are most motorcyclists that I have met; they like the historical associations of their machine, undeniably, and they like the look of it. That's the major difference between a HOG member and the owner of an expensive sports car: they like the look of it, *and not just the looks they are getting*. Think about any gathering of desirable motorcycles, from Daytona Beach to three Softails outside a bar. You may envy the owners, sure, and admire their custom treatments, but you are looking at the machinery. What you want to know about an XJ220 is who on earth owns it – and you know he's never going to drive it further than the electronic gates without armed outriders. If you are lucky enough to see a perfectly restored 1936 EL you will admire the owner's tenacity, but you won't really care if he's an accountant or an astronaut - you'll be looking at the funny ignition timer on the knucklehead engine. If the brilliant marketeers at Harley Davidson ever get to thinking that the image is everything and the product needs no development, 90 glorious years – some not too glorious – won't be worth a layer of lacquer.

The case against image, against outlaw/

cowboy/frontiersman associations as the prime mover behind the extraordinary recent success of the company, should not be overstated. A hundred examples, from film to song to superstar ownership can be cited, and some will be in this book. One for now, but not really with outlaw connections: in 1993 the auctioneers Sotheby's organized a sale at the Regensburg palace of Saint Emmeram in Germany for Princess Gloria von Thurn und Taxis. The proceeds were to help pay off estate duty following her husband's death. 3500 lots of furniture and works of art, 75,000 bottles of wine from the palace cellars and various other bric-a-brac helped to keep the $1.5bn family fortune intact. Alongside the marble and bronze statues and the silverware were two Harley-

LEFT: The Fat Boy, introduced in 1990, with alloy disc wheels, its own saddle bags and a superb pearl gray finish. And a great name for this machine, which is based upon the Heritage Softail. What you see is what you get: a big lump of touring metal with few (apparent) nods toward modern motorcycle technology.

LEFT: Uncle Sam actually had every reason to be grateful to Harley-Davidson in both World Wars: 7000 machines were produced for the First World War – far less than the 20,000 supplied by Indian, who sold to the government at a knockdown price which was eaten away by inflation – but more than 80,000 for the Second World War, mostly solo WLA 45 cu. in. models.

RIGHT: 1948 FL panhead, the new mill to replace the ten-year-old knucklehead. The new engine, with its aluminum alloy cylinder head and hydraulic lifters, was designed to overcome the problem of overheating that had plagued the earlier design. The new machine was not an immediate success: the lifters would not maintain the firing sequence if there was any variation in the oil pressure.

OVERLEAF: Richard Johnson's 1989 FLHTC Ultra Classic Tour Glide, with frame-mounted fairing, stereo, intercom, self-cancelling turn signals, cruise control and a five-gallon tank, all standard.

Davidsons belonging to the princess herself. *Of course* they were Harleys, somehow she could not possibly have owned a Kawasaki Z1, nor even a BMW. The princess was not pictured in the press waving the late Prince Albert's walking stick inlaid with rubies, but sitting astride one of Milwaukee's finest. And most tellingly – she owned not two, but three . . .

Harley-Davidson have been aware of the immense commercial importance of the aura surrounding the name, not just the myriad individual products, from the early days when dozens of American companies were battling for supremacy, and startling numbers of tiny British companies – hundreds – were looking for an entry into the infant motorcycle market, some of them in the USA. "There's good reason why a Harley-Davidson motorcycle is so distinct. It's because of a steadfast insistence on doing things our own way. When something works, we stick with it." Which year, from, say, 1920 to 1994, was this brochure copy written? Impossible to guess: actually it was 1989.

That copy introduces one further point concerning technological development. Most people – those with a rudimentary knowledge of the motorcycle industry – do not fall for the old myth of Harley-Davidson as something of a dinosaur, limping a decade behind the latest ideas from Europe or Japan, relying on the V-twin to pull through against the technically superior competition. The company has made two-

Ultra Classic Tour Glide

Ultra Classic Tour Glide
Ultra Classic

and four-strokes and boxer twins, Bill Harley's original design for the sprung front fork was a genuine advance, and the Softail suspension was a cunning piece of engineering, (albeit bought under license from outside). Way back in 1912 the company produced arguably the first effective motorcycle clutch with a free wheel unit, and Harley four-valve heads preceded the Japanese tidal wave – there are countless other examples of Harley-Davidson's ingenuity. In 1974 Ducati must have thought they were ahead of the game when they abandoned their successful line of 750 V-twins and introduced the 860 GTI. The brilliant designer Giorgetto Giugiaro was brought in to style the new machine, along with the new 350 and 500GTL parallel twins. Working to an almost impossible brief, whereby the motorcycles were supposed to appeal to just about everyone from the shopper to the speed freak, he produced a bitty, angular machine that looked ugly then and looks ugly now. Loyal Ducati fans deserted the marque in droves. Whether they did they do so because of the looks, or because of the fact that the 860 did not have Desmo valve gear, possessed by the high-performance, so-called "prototype" that had won the Barcelona 24-hour marathon the previous year, is a moot point.

This story is told to illustrate two points: the first is that the motorcycle-buying public is not easily conned by apparently intangible technical improvements, even those buyers who display fierce brand loyalty. The second is that the primary business law is to cultivate the customers you already have, or at the very least do not alienate them, before you attempt to plunder markets dominated by others. The sales of the new middle-weight Ducatis were just as bad: the Japanese were selling hundreds of thousands of middleweight motorcycles at the time. It's very easy for the eyes to glaze over when figures for Japanese production are quoted, but in 1974 nearly a fifth of all the motorcycles in the world were Honda CB350 twins. In its first production year, Honda sold 2,132,902 CX500s, as a mere

RIGHT: Some people are never satisfied. The standard lights on the FLH Electra Glide are quite adequate, but this owner has made sure that his machine just cannot be missed. Playing with the basic package is positively encouraged by the company – just so long as all the bells and whistles are officially licensed Harley-Davidson products.

BELOW: The FXST Softail was introduced in 1984, the Heritage Softail in the following year. It was an ingenious homage to the 1950s hardtail in looks, with gas horizontal rear shocks hidden under the transmission.

MOTOR
HARLEY-DAVIDSON
CYCLES
Harley-Davidson
NEW YORK
ART 2
MOTOR
HARLEY-DAVIDSON
CYCLES

ABOVE: **This is a "baby" Harley engine – that is a mere (FX 1980) 74 cu. in. The new engine for 1984, which is the most important development in H-D history in the last ten years, the Evo, would weigh in at a full 1340 cc.**

sideshow to the new CB360s. But Ducati still should have resisted: Ducati enthusiasts wanted sports bikes, just as they had for decades, and not "mediocrity with a dash of class" as *Cycle Illustrated* described the CB360.

Why is this relevant to Harley-Davidson, and more specifically, to the company's technological developments? It is relevant because for most of the time the company did resist, and still does resist, tarnishing its hard-won image by introducing new technology too soon, or too radically. There have been exceptions, of course: the 1929 74 cu.in. VL was something of a disaster at the outset, for example. Coming up to date, pre-1991 Sportsters had chain and battery problems, 1340s were recalled in the early nineties with suspect selector forks – even on the divine Electra Glide, exhaust heat shields have been known to drop off!

Nevertheless, the best metaphor for the Harley-Davidson company throughout much of its history is an immensely powerful man carrying a great load up a ladder, never moving a foot to the next rung until

LEFT: Custom Shovelhead Sportster cruises Red River. The Sportster name was first heard in 1957, and today the 883 Sportster provides an entry level machine. But for the Sportster, just as for the big twins, the engine capacity has inevitably grown.

BELOW: A softail color explosion. In recent years, the factory have improved the finish on all of the machines, but when you see a lineup like this of custom paint, it hardly seemed worth it.

RIGHT: The Harley-Davidson café, New York. There just had to be a place like this. If you have an icon revered throughout the world, it's bound to help you sell beer.

BELOW: Three miles of Harley-Davidsons *en route* from the fair grounds to the Summerfest. Events such as Sturgis and Daytona Bike Week are astoundingly well-attended, and help to cement loyalty to the marque of the HOG brotherhood.

that load is securely held. In 1924 they debated whether to introduce four-cylinder machines to compete with the Henderson and the Ace, particularly for the police market. Following considerable design effort William Davidson said no, as the tooling would have been too expensive, and concentrated on the J model V-twin. Earlier, in 1911, the problem was whether to put chain drives on the new 45-degree V-twins. No, they made the belt larger and were confident enough to offer the guarantees against defective parts already offered on the singles. And in 1983 there was a real problem with new emissions regulations, ease of maintenance wasn't what it was, the V-twin design was ancient – should we start again? Of course not. The company spent $15 million to develop an engine based on the old shovelhead bottom end, but with vastly superior heat dissipation, electronic ignition and fuel consumption. They called it "Evo." The Harley-Davidson feel was not sacrificed. Of course such caution means that Harley-Davidson are not in the vanguard when it comes to out-and-out performance. Today, Yamaha have won more world titles than any other marque in history. H-D have just four to their credit.

Can anyone remember the early eighties turbocharged Japanese machines? They probably seemed like a good idea at the time. Every major car manufacturer seemed to have at least one model using the "new" technology. Unfortunately, the turbo tended to get in on the action at the most inopportune moments, say, when accelerating out of a corner. Perhaps I couldn't ride it, but that desire to pirouette made me nervous on a Honda turbo 650. The 200 bhp turbos from Egli have probably sorted out the problem. *200 bhp*? Give me evolution, not revolution, every time. Give me the two-wheel Heartbeat of America.

BELOW LEFT: The reputation of the myriad chapters is forever distorted by the really bad guys, as described – accurately, it must be said – in Dr Hunter S. Thompson's celebrated book, *Hell's Angels*. Most HOG members are, of course, average law-abiding Joes with a love of motorcycles.

BELOW: Sturgis Main Street, cruising past the official Hell's Angel hangout, Gunner's Lounge.

CHAPTER ONE

BEGINNINGS

Putting some iron in the American Soul

"Speed Kills." But not always. One of the most remarkable aspects of the early history of Harley-Davidson is just how quickly a machinist, a student/draftsman, a patternmaker and a railroad toolmaker would become the President, Chief Engineer, Secretary/General Sales Manager and Works Manager of a company producing hundreds of machines a year, soon employing hundreds of people.

The machinist and the company's first president was Walter Davidson Sr. He worked for the Chicago, Milwaukee and St Paul Railroad until what had been his brother Arthur's hobby turned into a going concern. His business acumen would be vital – as would his win on a Harley-Davidson in the 1908 New York Endurance Run, which helped to set the name in the public consciousness for the first time. His financial abilities were highlighted by the fact that he would, in later years, become a trustee of the Northwestern Mutual Insurance Company and a director of the First Wisconsin bank. Try to invent your own president of a fledgling motorcycle company: an individual with business savvy, of course, but what a bonus to have a man who was an accomplished rider, and who could understand the tolerances of an engine.

The draftsman and then Chief Engineer was William S. Harley. Bill Harley was a bicycle fitter at the age of 15, clever enough to become an apprentice draftsman, who later studied engineering at the University of Wisconsin. His talents would produce many of the classic Harley-Davidson designs right up to the Second World War. Another natural for the team – oh, and incidentally another excellent competition rider.

The patternmaker turned Sales Manager was Arthur Davidson. So far we have a fine engineer and a money man with a firm grasp of the realities of production for our enterprise. What else do we need? A salesman. Every company knows that its product can be the best in the world, but without efficient distribution it will fail. In 1910 Arthur Davidson began to recruit a dealership network across the country. To be honest, he didn't have that much to work on at that time: brother Walter's 1908 endurance run success, a perfect score of 1000 points (plus an additional five complimentary points from the admiring organizers) in New York; and team victory in the 1909 FAM (Federation of American Motorcyclists) Endurance Run. Plus some pretty sturdy machines for sale. Do not forget that Indian and Excelsior were out there in the market place, and would sell more machines than Harley-Davidson for some time to come. This makes his success all the more praiseworthy. It was based upon a simple principle: that the dealer must be happy, which means that he must make money. Exclusive dealerships would be outlawed later – the legislation had actually been aimed at the car market – but that per-

RIGHT: A Harley-Davidson 61 cu.in. V-twin, circa 1915. The "V" configuration was first put together by Bill Harley in 1909. The pocket valve twin would be produced for the next ten years.

PREVIOUS PAGES: Walter Davidson, first president of the Harley-Davidson Motor Company. Walter had won the Federation of American Motorcyclists Endurance Run, garnering vital publicity for brother Arthur Davidson's efforts to establish a dealership network.

HARLEY-
DAVIDSON

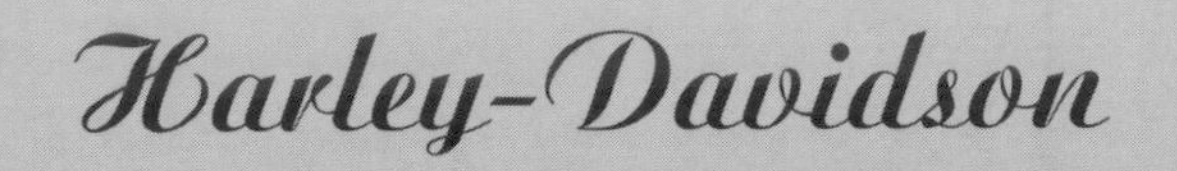

HARLEY-DAVIDSON 1903

The first Harley-Davidson, it was made by hand and based on the French De Dion motor. There was no gearbox and the rider had to push the machine up to compression and then pedal furiously until the engine fired.

Designations	n/a
Engine	De Dion-Bouton atmospheric inlet valve
Bore & stroke	3 × 3½ in.
Displacement	25 cu.in.
Suspension	unsprung forks
BHP	2
Top speed	approx. 25 mph

haps made the principle even more valid: a happy dealer would devote more of his time to the H-D product.

One more recruit for the cause: someone to oversee production. The railroad tool-maker and foreman who would become Works Manager was the eldest Davidson brother, William. He bought the production machinery required as the company grew faster than anyone could have predicted, and to do just that without a major mistake over 30 years is impressive enough, let alone attempt to ensure that the machines produced pass quality control and that the workforce is content. William was a paternal figure, who saw the company and its employees suffer through the Depression and, drawing his own conclusions from that experience, was opposed to the introduction of the union, which happened in 1937,

days before his death.

Just about the only way to improve on this team, in business, technical and production terms, is to make it a close-knit one. Make them brothers, and friends. (Arthur Davidson and Bill Harley were schoolfriends and had worked together in Milwaukee's Barth Manufacturing Company.) It would also be useful, if we are creating a legend, to ensure longevity with a second, even a third generation: William H. Davidson would join his father's company in 1928, Gordon Davidson would enter on the sales side, then there was Bill Harley's brother John, William J. Harley, and today grandson Willie G. This friendly, family team it seemed, just could not fail.

Of course it could. In the first place, the whole thing might never have happened. The first machine which Walter put together from Arthur's patterns and Bill's designs, with a De Dion-type single cylinder engine, was not produced for sale, simply for fun. Secondly, the necessary technical information about the engine was provided by Emil Kruger, a German immigrant working at the Barth Manufacturing Company with Arthur and Bill. Similarly, marine engineer designer Ole Evinrude just happened to live near the Davidson household, and would help with carburetor development. Thirdly, and most importantly, no one at the turn of the century could have predicted that a combustion engine which turned a wheel could provide genuine two-wheel transport, rather than just an expensive toy, and was therefore a means of income for a family man with a responsible job, like Bill Davidson. There were other people out there insane enough to try it anyway, so it wasn't as if there was a clear field even if you did succeed in making the machines. The whole enterprise could have fallen apart at the very beginning. It didn't because the company's founders were bound together by a fascination with engineering and because none

ABOVE: The motorcycle frame was originally based upon the bicycle frame, an apparently logical step which would cause no end of trouble for the designers of the fledgling industry. Harley-Davidson would actually produce their own bicycles in years to come, but the effort was not a success.

Harley-Davidson

SILENT GRAY FELLOW 1905

Available from 1904-18, the Silent Gray Fellow was revolutionary, not in its design, but in its durability.

Designations	5-35, 9A, 9B, 9E
Engine	De Dion-Bouton atmospheric inlet valve to 1910, pocket valve until 1918
Bore & stroke	3 × 3½ in.
Displacement	35 cu.in.
Suspension	leading line forks
BHP	6.5
Top speed	45 mph (claimed)

of the participants immediately gave up the day job, a wise decision and somehow symbolic of the cautious Harley-Davidson ethos over the following decades.

Two machines were made in 1904, eight in 1905. The company was finally incorporated in 1907, after some 150 machines had been sold, a healthy number which boded well for the future. All had been put together in a tiny shed in the back yard of the Davidson home at 38th and Highland Boulevard. The reason why they had sold well was improved reliability. There were similar sheds all over the USA, and some – maybe a little bigger – in the UK. The machines they were producing were often expensive (a fact often overlooked) and featured a dazzling array of engine "improvements".

The market for powered bicycles had been stimulated by the popularity of pedal cycle racing on board tracks and the consequent need for powered pacemakers. But that was at the very root of the problem. Plenty of people were looking at the petrol engine, tweaking it and attaching it in various ways to pedal cycle frames. Bill Harley was astute enough to abandon early on the old and unsatisfactory diamond-shaped frame and replace it with a looped frame better suited to the stresses involved. The frame was not a radical departure – it followed what was best practice around at the time – but the integrated package was well-thought-out, better balanced than machines with similar design considerations. The original De Dion engine was uprated from 2⅛ × 2⅞ in. bore and stroke, too weak for all but the gentlest gradients, to 3 × 3½ in., a change only made possible by use of the new frame. Still no tire scorcher, but it didn't blow up. The front fork was heavy gauge and the wheels were unusually strong and heavy. In short, reliability, not speed, was the watchword.

Bill Harley went off to study at the University of Wisconsin, but had time to design the Harley sprung front fork which would feature for several years; typically, an excellent design so long as the machine wasn't ridden too fast. By 1908, the famous shed had been outgrown, finance had been secured and a new, brick-built factory on Juneau Avenue with 18 employees produced 450 machines. The single-cylinder machine, with a very good muffler, produced between 1904 and 1918, became known as the "Silent Gray Fellow" in the advertising copy. Yes, there was advertising copy: the company was very quick to realize the importance of sales literature, and in fact the history of Harley-Davidson advertising is a fascinating one, running alongside the products themselves, following the same highs and lows.

The single-cylinder 5-35 model was significantly improved in 1909; the engine was upped to 35 cu.in. giving 5 hp, magneto ignition was introduced, and the frame was lengthened. But something much more sig-

Harley-Davidson

SIXTY-ONE 1909

Harley-Davidson's first V-twin survived until 1929

Designations	F, FE, J, JE, JD, JDH
Engine	4-stroke pocket valve twin
Bore & stroke	3 × 3½ in.
Displacement	61 cu.in.
Suspension	springer front forks
BHP	7
Top speed	approx. 50 mph

HARLEY-DAVIDSON

"The Motor Cycle Magnificent."

Write for Name and Address of nearest Agent

All models now being delivered

Model 20J, electrically equipped.

HARLEY-DAVIDSON MOTOR CO., LIMITED,
74, Newman Street, London, W.1

LEFT: A 1920 British advertisement for the Sixty-One, a sturdy, downright sensible design, enough to survive in production for 20 years.

ABOVE: **You don't see many of those on the road these days. The roller chain was first introduced in 1912 to replace the leather belt, when Bill Harley had solved the problem of clutch control with his "freewheeling" rear wheel mechanism.**

nificant also happened that year: Bill Harley took two 5-35 cylinders on a common crankshaft and arranged them at a 45-degree angle. At the same time the "ioe" (inlet-over-exhaust) valve, which became known as the "pocket valve" replaced the old atmospheric inlet valve which had survived from the original De Dion design. The V-twin configuration limits the cylinder bore size because of the angles, which means almost inevitably a long stroke, slow turning engine, which produces plenty of torque. Piston speeds over 4000 rpm would result in vibration, because of the uneven firing sequence, so ultimate power development must be limited: lower revs, however, make for a longer-lasting engine. The lazy beat of the Harley-Davidson, a sound which other manufacturers have tried – and failed – to emulate, was heard for the first time. Capacity was 61 cu.in. Only a handful of V-twins were produced in 1909, and none in 1910, because the mechanical inlet valves were not yet in place, but the four-stroke pocket valve twin – the "Sixty-One" would be produced for the next ten years. In 1912 the rear hub clutch cited in the introduction was introduced, alongside chain drive to replace the old belts. As a reminder of what riding a motorcycle was really all about on the rutted roads of the period, one of the most welcome innovations was a saddle mounted on a sprung seat pillar. In 1914 the rider could, for the first time, start his engine

LEFT: Model J, 1915, photographed at Danbury, Ct. The center post saddle had been a welcome innovation three years previously, the "Full-Floating Seat" making life a little more bearable on the unmetalled or badly maintained roads.

BELOW: The Flying Merkel V-twin racers split the Harley and Indian competition in the 1910s.

RIGHT: For 1915, the J benefited from an all-enclosed three speed sliding gear transmission, far more effective for sidecar work. Power had been upped considerably since the V-twin of 1909, by improvements to breathing and valves.

Harley-Davidson

J-11 1915

The inlet-over-exhaust layout remained in use on the big twins until 1929.

Engine	ioe V-twin
Bore & stroke	3 × 3½ in.
Displacement	60 cu. in.
Suspension	leading link forks
BHP	11
Top speed	60 mph

simply by stepping on either foot pedal, which must have seemed quite startlingly sophisticated. A two-speed transmission and carburetor choke were also introduced in that year.

"Racing improves the breed" must be one of the most dangerously seductive ideas ever to be applied in any branch of the automotive industry. Winning at Le Mans didn't seem to increase minuscule production figures at Aston Martin, and it didn't keep the wolf from the door at Bentley (except that it did manage to attract vast sums of money from the flamboyant millionaire Wolf Barnato). Sometimes of course, it works, and knowledge gained and advertising garnered from competition can help the production models immeasurably. Norton is the obvious two-wheel example. In the case of the two-speed gearbox, the abject failure of two privately-entered Harleys in the 1913

San Diego-Phoenix Desert Race may have galvanized the company into providing a decent 'box for the V-twin. Typically, Harley-Davidson were not seduced by competition from the beginning. Finally, in 1914, William Ottaway was employed as assistant to Bill Harley to look at works racing. Following a few tentative outings in that year, Otto Walker won the Venice, California road race in 1915 and once again in Dodge City, with a modified V-twin. Racing success would continue right up to US entry into the First World War, Single cylinders were prepared for ½-mile dirt track racing, and hemispherical combustion chamber 8-valve engines designed for 1916.

Three speeds became available on the road machines in 1915, with an enclosed sliding gear design, again, state-of-the-art. The teen years of this century were wonderful for motorcycle manufacturers in the USA. More than 30 companies were achieving more than acceptable turnover every year, led by what would become Harley's greatest rival and eventually, scalp, Indian. The war would be a boost, not a problem, at least for Harley-Davidson. The factory was expanding all the time, and by 1915 more than 1500 were employed . By 1918, with war orders on the books, the company was the largest motorcycle manufacturer in the world. Arthur Davidson penetrated the utility market, selling large numbers of machines for use in rural mail delivery, where reliability and strength was all, to police departments and to the Bell Telephone Company. There was a large enough market for everyone: the specter of Mr Ford's mass transport revolution had not yet been glimpsed. Sidecars and other accessories helped to boost profits. The utility aspect of the motorcycle explosion is the subject of the next chapter. ''Utility'', as in dependability, was the bottom line in the Flanders mud.

BELOW: The Harley-Davidson inlet-over-exhaust (ioe) V-twin engine, *circa* 1917. Despite production of other engine configurations for decades to come, it would always be the V-twin that was the bedrock of the company.

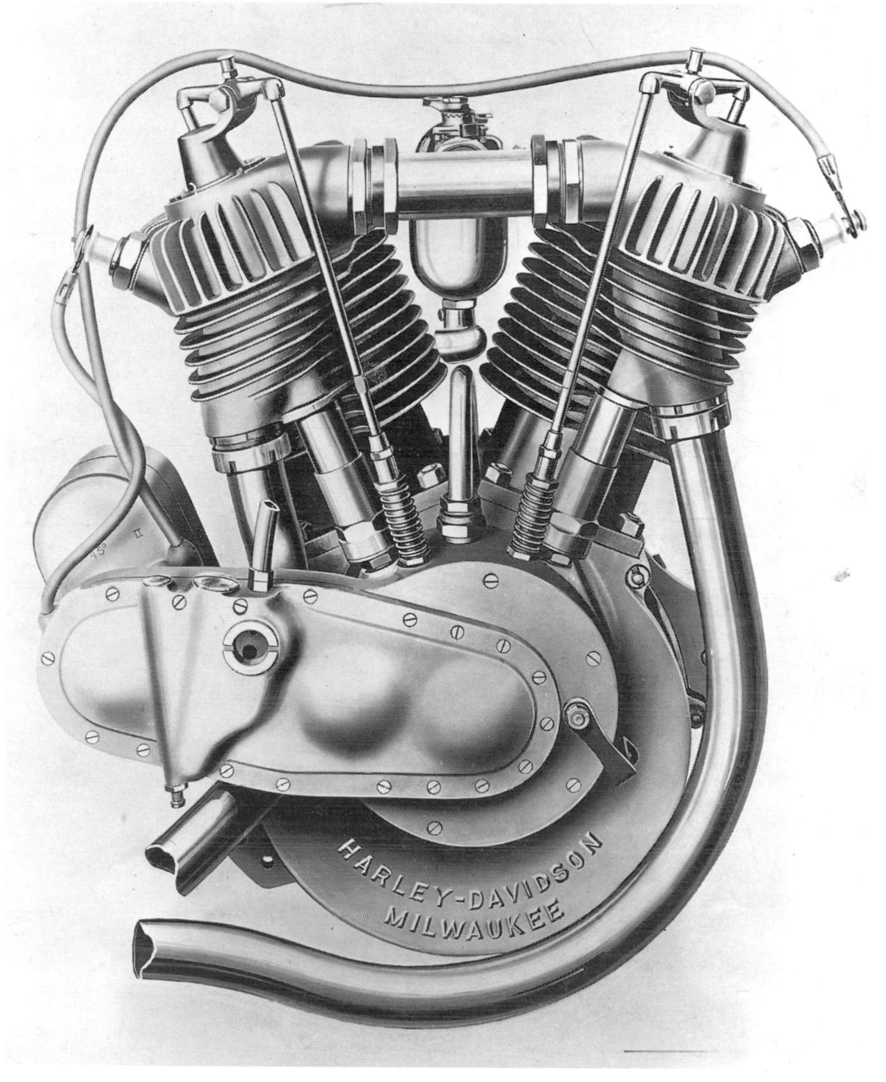

CHAPTER TWO

HARLEYS IN UNIFORM

In 1913, Indian produced over 31,000 of the 71,000 machines made in the USA, far and away the market leader. What happened? Why is the marque (at the time of writing anyway) a welcome addition to a classic bike gathering, but nothing more? Part of the answer is found in the decision of the directors to offer 20,000 machines, on a perilously tight margin, (which would evaporate under wartime inflation) to the government for service in the Great War. It certainly would not damage the company disastrously, but it would loosen its hold on the production machine market. As Indian transferred to military production, Harley-Davidson took a long, cold look, offered 7000 machines and set about improving their own dealer network. It would be a different story in 1941. The H-D 45 prepared by Bill Harley was practically ready for wartime service a year before Pearl Harbor: eventually, more than 80,000 machines would be supplied, together with enough spares for 30,000 more. A careful look around the countryside of France will reveal some of these machines still on active service, with old French farm workers sensitive to the mechanical needs of such venerable warhorses. The 45s, while of course not having the cachet of the big Harleys in the restorer's market, gain more and more admirers as time passes.

There are other kinds of uniform involved here, not just olive drab. By 1914, nine federal departments were on Harleys. Arthur Davidson's trip to the 1909 annual convention of the Rural Free Delivery Mail Carriers of America in Chicago had paid off five years later to the tune of nearly 5000 machines. In 1915, the company offered a side delivery van which was sold to companies with their logos and names painted on.

The relationship between Harley-Davidson and the police has been a long and fruitful one. Nowadays, the Business Development Police and Fleet Sales section of the company produce a fine little magazine called *The Mounted Officer* to help maintain those links forged 80 years previously. The California Highway Patrol have been known to sit astride Kawasakis, but that unfortunate lapse has now been more or less corrected. Ducati, Moto-Guzzi, BMW and others have all made inroads into this particular niche market, but H-D are still in there fighting. Before the Great War, Indian, naturally, had a stranglehold on the business, together with Excelsior. The four-cylinder Excelsior machines did not vibrate as much as the Harley-Davidsons, so were more comfortable over a long day spent chasing speeding car drivers, or maybe fleeing horses. Strong four-cylinder competition also appeared from the Henderson and the Ace. In 1924 the company looked long and hard at producing their own four-cylinder specifically for the market, but William Davidson was reluctant to disturb the production of the J model, and he was probably right.

PREVIOUS PAGES: 80 cu. in. FLHTP's on duty with the Houston PD. The competition to supply motorcycles to police departments has always been fierce, not to say cut-throat. Harley-Davidson have always been aware of the contribution of such multiple sales not only to turnover but also to the public's attitude to the company's products.

RIGHT: Harley-Davidson's major contribution to the European theater of the Second World War: the side-valve 45 cu. in. WLA.

MILITARY POLICE
3A
2ΔP
HQ 5
SHIP.WGT.-535LBS
O-LGTH-88INS
O-HT-59INS
O-WIDTH-37INS

ABOVE: Harleys were offered to police departments at very competitive rates. This is a typical 1916 squad.

RIGHT: So what's in the box? Actually it's a heavyweight set of scales with which this patrolman checked the autos and trucks for overloading on the highways of Illinois in the early 1930s. The 45 D series was just the ticket for issuing tickets.

By 1925, H-D had supplied machines to about 2500 police departments. But there was no doubt that the motorcycles from the competition were quicker. Because cars as mass transport were a new phenomenon, the authorities were caught on the hop as the death toll mounted through the "roaring" decade. What would eventually make the Harley-Davidson the machine of choice was the gradual improvement in performance of the V-twins, and the company's relentless pursuit of the market. As described in Chapter Four, Harley-Davidson would offer the police version VL direct to the public at a very low price to stave off some of the dire financial consequences of the Depression, sparking a deadly war with Indian, and would, at the beginning of the 1930s, have expanded the network to 3000 police departments. Dealers didn't like selling to the police much, as they often negotiated servicing clauses and punitive buy-back options. There was little choice but to accept the terms demanded by the bulk buyers, however, and it needs little imagination to realize that graft must have colored some of those deals.

The twins were finally accepted as not fast, but fast enough for everyday police work: the indefatiguable clutch, the workhorse gearbox and drive line (especially in comparison with the more fragile Indian twin) slowly won the day. Most police work is not tank-slapping chases after Al Capone, but cruising the highways and crawling through the city – today as then. And this, as any Harley-Davidson fan knows, is just what the big V-twins do best. The company also knew the advertising power of the Man on a Harley-Davidson machine, and has exploited it from the 1920s to the present day. "Let HIM stop the Wave of Killings," they trumpeted in 1930. "Give the Motorcycle Policeman the job of curbing motor fatalities in your community . . . Curb Autocides."

V-twins were still supplied to police departments during the Second World War, when almost all production was of 45s, and after VJ Day the 74 cu.in. FL in low compression form was king of the highway patrols. The hand gearchange, the comfort at low speed and the general look of the machine (the latter especially important for escort duties) won the day. By the 1970s of course, the Japanese manufacturers were snapping at the company's heels, in this market as in others. In the AMF era, not only did Harley-Davidsons sport Japanese forks, shocks and carburetors, but highway patrolmen could be seen lurking behind advertising hoardings on Hondas! The Evo engines would storm the police market again in the 1980s, with the FXRTP as the main weapon, and sales are good now. The

STATE OF ILLINOIS
HIGHWAY PATROL

RIGHT: This is actually an ex-police 1940 61 cu. in. EL, that knucklehead engine obviously now in loving private hands; (at the time this picture was taken, those of Mr B. Gagne).

HARLEY-DAVIDSON

ABOVE: Another ex-police model now in private ownership (Joe "Oz" Osborne), this time a panhead 1960 Duo-Glide. There was no electric start for the FL or the FLH until 1965.

California Highway Patrol required a top speed of 100 mph, and got it in 1984 with a new fairing.

You can hang a lot of things on a big twin, which did not escape the notice of the police departments, or of the company. Just as H-D realized the importance of aftermarket sales in the civilian market of the 1920s, and milked it with a tinge of understandable desperation in the 1930s, so the accessory list specifically for police machines is very long. Optional lexan windshield, hazard warning tell tales, siren, radio static suppression kit, the official H-D police jacket, plus, of course, all the extra chrome that the civilian can get "to enhance resale value", the muffler, battery covers, etc. Sometimes in the long history of the patrolman and his Harley-Davidson, the machines were sold at a very low price, a sacrifice made necessary to compete with the Moto-Guzzis and "tailor-made" motorcycles such as the 1975

LEFT AND BELOW: It's just as well that the man is on the right machine come Sturgis party time. The patrolmen are provided with a few of those extras from the accessory list mentioned on the page opposite. Count them off.

RIGHT: **The FLHT Electra Glide in service, Houston. No Hondas or Kawasakis here. American iron has been ridden by American police departments since 1907.**

Harley-Davidson

Kawasaki KZp Police Special. It was a sacrifice that anyone who has seen the Houston officers out on their FLHTPs is happy about.

Let slip the hogs of war. In 1916, Pancho Villa, the Mexican revolutionary, murdered a number of American engineers. President Wilson sent an armed force under General Pershing to capture him. The War Department had been in possession of motorcycles with mounted machine guns for some time, but not Harley-Davidsons. When the order came, the company jumped. Two days later, the first dozen machines were at the border, ready for General "Black Jack" Pershing. And just about as quickly, the advertising copy was printed: "Uncle Sam now has 34 Harley-Davidsons in Mexican frontier service." The sidecar gun carriage mounted a Colt machine gun.

Despite the company's canny reservation of machines for the civilian market, the number of Harley-Davidson machines supplied for the First World War was still very high as a percentage of overall production. By the end of the war, *all* new Harleys going down the line were for military service. One spinoff from the conflict for the company was that British civilian production was suspended before US entry into the war, so that British riders had to look to the American manufacturers. This opened up the market and would provide a peace dividend of sorts, though other events would overtake the company, and indeed the industry as a whole.

Different sources quote different figures for the number of machines actually shipped overseas. The interesting point is that those Harley-Davidson singles and twins that did cross the Atlantic were not modified in any appreciable way. When peace came, the design was unchanged for the civilian market, which meant there was no need to sell unshipped machines as war surplus. (Though of course hard-ridden machines were sold off after the Armistice.) Even the olive green paint job remained the same, for the next 15 years in fact. Before official US entry into the war in 1917, Harley-Davidsons were already in England ferrying wounded soldiers to hospitals across the country. Most machines were employed in scouting or messenger service rather than actual combat. Think of the reality of that awful, static war of attrition and this becomes obvious. Norton advertising of the time shows brave Tommies flying across open country, machine-guns blazing, and such a wartime image is more comforting than the reality of field ambulance units.

Massive vehicle depots were set up at home, as they were for the Second World War, and it soon became apparent that maintenance would become a problem. The Army needed help to exploit the hardware properly and got it in the form of the first Harley-Davidson Service School, established in 1917 to train military personnel in

BELOW: The first use of Harley-Davidsons by the US military, on the hunt for Pancho Villa in 1916. They didn't find him, but it did the company's reputation no harm at all.

ABOVE: August 6, 1918; an H-D mounted messenger awaits delivery of photographic plates from observer Lt. J. H. Snyder, to take them to the field studio for developing. The pilot was Major J. N. Reynolds of the 91st Aero Squadron, Gondreville-sur-Moselle.

LEFT: The first class of pupils at the US Army's Harley-Davidson school, 1917.

basic maintenance. A more comprehensive training was given over a three-week course actually at the plant. The first course, in July 1917, was taken by nine corporals from Fort Sam Houston. The regular school continued in peacetime, another intelligent development by the company: the more people who know how to service your machines, the better in terms of aftermarket care and thus reputation. More than 300 enlisted repairmen followed the course, but fortunately peace came before the US was fully mobilized and only a few had to make the trip. Most were posted to army camps

USA

with consignments of machines.

The most famous Harley-Davidson story to come out of the First World War would probably have been lost for all time, were it not for an unknown photographer. It deserves retelling. On November 8th, 1918, with everyone drunk on the possibility of an end to the war, Corporal Roy Holtz from Chippawa Falls, Wisconsin was ordered out on a night mission. Corporal Holtz was a dispatch rider, and his mount was a Harley-Davidson with sidecar. The destination that night for the corporal and the captain riding with him is unclear, but it wasn't reached. The roads of northern Belgium were a sea of mud and the night shattered by artillery fire, which obviously did nothing for the captain's sense of direction in the dark. Holtz knew the countryside well and told the captain that they were traveling in the wrong direction – toward enemy lines. The captain was having none of it, so they pressed on. When they stopped to ask directions at a farmhouse, it became abundantly clear that they had, indeed, been traveling east, not west: the farmhouse was a German divisional headquarters. Both were captured by German officers from a Bavarian division. Holtz could speak fluent German and was treated to a drink, perhaps in an attempt to loosen his tongue, although it is hard to believe that any German soldier at that late stage would have been interested in military intelligence, unless it was advice on where best to surrender. The pair were held until the morning of November 11, Armistice Day, and then released to make their way back to the Allied lines. Somehow they separated – and that in itself might make an interesting story – maybe it's for the best that the name of the over-confident captain is not known, or at least not published.

The reason why we know the name of Roy Holtz is that as he finally returned westward, through retreating Germans, a German civilian took a picture of an unusual sight. It is a haunting image: shadowy figures of a supply column turn to watch the passing rider, goggles pushed back on the top of his head, spare tire around the nose

OPPOSITE: A trusty warhorse, long in the tooth now, but still on the move. It is not so unusual to see a WLA in the possession of a venerable French farmer today, rumbling along the lanes of Normandy. The leather saddle bags were part of the original military specification.

BELOW: Many WLA models have been converted to "rat bikes."

of the empty sidecar. The picture was found by another dispatch rider in a German photography shop just a few days later and sent back to Harley-Davidson. The photograph was reproduced worldwide: "the first Yank to enter Germany," although he was actually leaving Germany at the time. *The Enthusiast* magazine had been established in 1916 to further the Harley cause, and is still published today, making it the world's oldest continuously published motorcycle magazine. In 1943 they published the picture of the unknown soldier who duly turned up at Juneau Avenue to obtain a copy and tell his story.

Between the wars Harley-Davidsons entered military service under various colors. Notably the "Rikuo" (which translates roughly as "king of the road") twins manufactured under license in Japan until as late as 1946. The Harley-Davidson connection with the Japanese war machine was not featured in *The Enthusiast*. Machines were sold in Central America, South America, Mongolia and saw action in

BELOW: US Airborne infantry in training, 1944. The rider descends from a fuselage mockup.

LEFT: Just to make sure that the boys behave themselves while they're "over there". A phalanx of Harley-Davidson mounted MPs pose for posterity in Whitehall, London.

BELOW: A Canadian motorcyclist causes a stir in the grounds of a country house in southern England used as a brigade HQ. The WLAC used the front forks and brakes from the bigger twins. Note the pillion saddle and auxiliary box on top of the front mudguard.

Harley-Davidson

FORTY-FIVE WLA 1941

During the Second World War nearly 80,000 WLAs were produced for the Allies.

Designations	WLA, WLAC (Canada)
Engine	side-valve V-twin
Bore & stroke	2¾ × 3^{13}⁄$_{16}$ in.
Displacement	45 cu. in.
Suspension	leading link forks
BHP	23
Top speed	65 mph

U.S.

the Spanish Civil War. The distinction between police and military use was blurred in some countries.

In 1937, four years before Pearl Harbor, the Army inspected the civilian service school. Everything was running smoothly; the Milwaukee school was fully capable of turning out 50 mechanics a month. Just as before the First World War, the motorcycle industry would be given clearance as essential war work and therefore would not be starved of the necessary materials. At the end of the 1930s, tests were carried out on purpose-built three-wheelers and combinations for cross-country utility, but were not deemed satisfactory by the military: enter the Willys Jeep.

In the fall of 1939, an order for 5000 solo machines came from Britain, following the bombing of the Triumph factory in Coventry. H-D provided a strengthened version of the old WLD 45, designated the WLA. 18-inch wheels, wider fenders, a bash plate under the crankcase and rear chain, a low compression modified WL-type engine with large air filter and more cooling fin area, a heavy luggage rack and a carbine bucket running down the front forks, all made for an excellently-adapted machine. So well-adapted in fact, that many would survive the war and are still grinding comfortably along in low gear today. It wasn't only Britain that received Harleys: the Russians too, looked to the USA as their ability to produce machines for themselves disappeared. In the final push for Berlin, the Russians reputedly rode west through Eastern Germany on 30,000 Harleys. With the British contract fulfilled, Harley-Davidson was given an open-ended contract by the US

BELOW: This trooper is one of a special squad undergoing training with a US company in Australia. Harley-Davidson's involvement in the Pacific War was very limited.

ABOVE: A member of a reconnaissance unit shows how it should be done in theory during battle training, England, February 24, 1943.

LEFT: Private Wilburn L. Cummings flies over a shell hole obstacle course in England. It wasn't only Harleys that saw service in the Second World War, of course. Nortons, BSAs and Triumphs also saw action, as well as Indian 741As and Bs, developed from the 500cc Junior and 750cc Scout respectively.

LEFT: If Hitler could have outriders for his Mercedes, so could the Finns for their Harley-Davidsons!

RIGHT: The French prepare to return home in 1944, somewhere in southern England. It's Harley-Davidson that will get them there.

BELOW: Essential information, perhaps even more vital for the Finns pictured above, and for the thousands of Harley-Davidson-mounted Russians.

ABOVE: Escorting the General, April 1944. Two Allies, two machines.

Defense Department for military machines. The company immediately expanded the production facilities and took on extra workers at Juneau Avenue.

Most production was taken up with the WLA, but some 74-in. and side-valve twin sidecars were supplied. The WLAC (for Canada) was an adaptation of the WLA for Canadian forces, with the front forks and brake from the larger twins, and a foot gear change on the right. The luggage rack could take a 40-lb radio and there was an additional luggage box on top of the front fender.

A much rarer bird was the XA horizontal twin – only about a thousand or so were built. It was designed specifically for the sands of North Africa, and its square bore and stroke was a steal from the BMW flat twins which seemed so at home in that hostile terrain. Unfortunately, the lubrication system was not a steal from the German design and bearings collapsed far too readily. When the war switched entirely to the East, the Jeep was king.

Not surprisingly, considering the enormous numbers of machines produced, there were plenty left over in 1945. 15,000 WLAs were up for sale in 1945. But what of the machines that did see active service? The figure of 30,000 machines rolling toward Berlin quoted above gives one of the simplest answers to the question of their employment – troop transportation, pure and simple. But the four main roles were as scouts, as a kind of traffic control for troop movements, able to move up and down the lines and relay information, the old courier employment of the Great War, and actual, commando-like attack. "The mounts of the 1942 Rough Riders, toughest and fastest of land-army troops," as they were described in *This Week* magazine, actually supported the armored divisions in battle, but mostly in the first three roles, not the last.

In 1943 the Harley-Davidson was presented with the Army-Navy "E" award for exceptional performance in the production of war materials. And rightly so. The effort was massive by all of the company's employees, including those at the very top. In February 1942 Walter Davidson died, aged 65, still at the helm of the company he helped to create. In 1944, Bill Harley died. So the postwar return to civilian production would be achieved without these two key members of the original Harley-Davidson family.

That story will be taken up in the following chapters. This foray into uniform has taken the narrative too far forward. The development through the 1920s and survival of the marque through the Depression must first be examined; and the ability to produce great machines at the most extraordinary times must be enjoyed.

BELOW: Following the Second World War, Harley-Davidsons continued in military service across the globe, from Belgium to South Africa. This Libyan MP was lucky enough to be provided with a Duo-Glide, pictured here in 1954.

LEFT: Dispatch riders of Signals units of a Canadian Division are inspected by senior Canadian officers during the visit of Lieutenant-General Sir H. C. E. Weymiss CB DSO MC of the British Army.

BELOW: Sgt. Joseph A. De Marco from New York receives intelligence from MPs at Les Champs de Losque, France, prior to the drive to Coutances, 1944.

CHAPTER THREE

THE ROARING TWENTIES

HARLEY-
DAVIDSON

To be strictly accurate, we take up the story in 1919. The company looked to be in good shape postwar, and so did the motorcycle market. In 1919 an almost incredible 23,000 motorcycles and 16,000 sidecars were produced. The old 61 had been improved steadily and in that year took a giant leap forward with the J model having its own home-grown electrical system for the first time, and battery/coil ignition. The big news that year was the Sport Twin. It was a solo machine with a horizontally opposed 37cu.in. 6hp engine. This was a real departure for the company. The final drive chain was enclosed and the frame was very light. The machine weighed just 274lb, without fuel. It wasn't a stayer in production terms, disappearing just four years later, but its reputation as a smooth, enjoyable motorcycle was unsurpassed.

1920 saw production figures climb again, and the company began to prepare for a huge expansion of capacity. Single cylinder production ceased, so that all efforts could be directed toward the larger and more profitable lines.

Disaster loomed in the form of the Model T Ford which cost $400, and had plenty of room inside. The two-seater was just $265. How could a noisy, cumbersome V-twin possibly compete with a family car? Hindsight is the best view to have of any radical reversal of course, but it is a little surprising that H-D had not foreseen the magnitude of the problem earlier. Henry Ford's dealership network was huge after all, and you can't set that up in secret. Harley-Davidson production figures for 1921 were about a third what they had been the previous year. Machines which had once been desired by a vast segment of the population were now regarded as second-best; the market had shrunk to the working man, probably outside the towns, and the enthusiast. To compound the problem, Indian was still a serious threat, despite their own huge overcapacity. Of course it wasn't just the Model T's inherent superiority which caused the slump in the motorcycle market: the automobile industry had overproduced and both Ford and GM were dumping products on to the market. The economy had overheated in the postwar celebrations, with the banks lending too much, for too much expansion. One angle of attack for H-D, and for the industry as a whole was to clean up its act. Harley-Davidson pulled out of competition, partly to save money, but also partly to disassociate the product from the danger of the tracks. Walter Davidson pledged his support for the dealers through these difficult times, and urged them to provide better aftersales service.

This certainly helped in the domestic market, but the saving grace of the company in the immediate mini-slump was its overseas network of dealers. In 1920, the company was represented in 67 countries worldwide, by more than 2000 dealers, the fruits of Arthur Davidson's earlier efforts.

PREVIOUS PAGES: 1927 74 cu. in. JD twin, in production from 1922 to the end of the decade. Bill Harley had contracted Arthur Constantine to redesign the J in 1925. He lowered the frame and replaced the old tank in a fairly successful attempt to update without really spending any money.

RIGHT: 1923 61 cu. in. model J. The first 74 cu. in. engine had appeared the year before, in part to fulfil the demand for greater power from sidecar users.

HARLEY-
DAVIDSON
MADE IN U.S.A

ABOVE: A brave attempt to explore a different engine configuration; but the word "Sport" was wholly inappropriate.

Harley-Davidson

SPORT TWIN 1919

Harley-Davidson's least successful early model, its lack of power made it unpopular and it was withdrawn in 1922.

Designations	W, WJ
Engine	horizontally opposed 4-stroke twin
Bore & stroke	$2\frac{3}{4} \times 3$ in.
Displacement	37 cu.in.
Suspension	springer front forks
BHP	6
Top speed	approx. 40 mph

LEFT: 1922 Sport Twin with owner Don Werner – a relatively rare machine in standard trim. The Sport Twin really wasn't such a bad machine for the utility rider, but the Indian Scout had better torque – and of course it didn't look so suspicious, as a V-twin.

BELOW: The optimism felt throughout the motorcycle industry at the beginning of the 1920s was ill-founded, and here's one very good reason why: the Ford T Model (this tourer is actually from 1916). The fact that Ford and GM would overproduce massively and practically dump stock at cost didn't help.

Prewar, perhaps as much as a sixth of Harley production had gone overseas. In the early 1920s, as much as 50 percent was shipped out. Europe was still recovering from the ravages of the war, and was way behind the United States in terms of consumer expectations, to say the least. Duncan Watson in the UK had been a key importer before the war, and was to be so again, co-ordinating imports across Europe. (Unfortunately, part of the export lifeline was cut in 1925 when import tax of 33⅓ percent was imposed by Britain.) Japan was also a profitable market, although one which would become a little more complex in the following decade.

Back in the United States, economy of operation was stressed in the advertising

LEFT: An unusual Harley-Davidson stunt for combination and pillion passenger: assistant professionals Fred Sladden and Johnny Raimondi broke the record for the number of holes played in a day – 263 in 16 hours 12 minutes at the Dunedin Isles Golf and Country Club, Florida. Presumably their mode of transport helped.

copy and in 1925 the 21-CD single cylinder was introduced with the commercial market firmly targeted. The smaller machine was successful at home and abroad. Perhaps the code names of the sidecars produced in this crisis period give some clue to the attitude of the company: in 1920, the "Joy" and in 1921 the "Meadow"; but in 1922 the "Plot" and in 1923 the "Purity" and "Puritan". The sidecars were still vital to turnover, so in 1922 the 74 cu.in. 18hp Superpowered Twin had been sensibly offered. From 1925 Harley were obliged to manufacture their own sidecars as their suppliers, the Rogers Company, ceased production in favor of more profitable contracts.

The emphasis on economy paid off in the

ABOVE: Off-side view of Dr L. Friedman's JD, taken at Daytona. Some restorers of such machines feel the need to fit a later front brake assembly to put their minds at ease when using their venerable irons today.

utility market. By 1924 1400 police departments were on Harley-Davidson machines. The J V-twin continued to evolve: the frame was lowered which gave a pleasantly racy, modern feel and the olive drab was (temporarily) abandoned in favor of "brewster" green enlivened with gold striping. "It's here! The sensational Stream-Line." The teardrop tank, so much a feature of Harley-Davidson, was introduced in 1925. The new design was by Arthur Constantine, commissioned by Bill Harley. It is a feature of Bill Harley's career that he would always know when outside help was needed. This is a virtue and not, as some have interpreted it, a fault.

A bonus was the failure of small accessories suppliers in the mini-slump: Harley had the money and distribution network to step straight into the gap. To find a gap in the H-D official accessories catalog today, you would need an extremely thin shim. At first, the problem of producing their own lighting sets, speedos and other paraphernalia was just an additional headache, but it soon began to turn a profit for the company and the dealers. Pressure was brought to bear on the dealers to ensure that only "official" accessories were available. Harry V. Sucher in his excellent book, *Harley-Davidson The Milwaukee Marvel*, points out a painful example. As power increased for the J models, so stress became a problem on the cam followers, but the company certainly was not going to mess around with the traditional valve cam configuration. Some riders and dealers soon discovered that Indian cam followers did not wear in the same way, and could be fitted without too much trouble. The result was dire warnings from head office to all dealers about this practice, which were often ignored, and a slightly half-hearted attempt to solve the problem with thicker metal.

In 1924 Walter Davidson devised a hire-purchase plan to attract new blood, and the dealers were encouraged to organize rallies to keep the converted happy, and hopefully hungry for new machines. But that was not enough to stave off a loss that year: not a big one, but the only one before things got really interesting in the following decade.

In 1928 the J lineup saw two new models with twin cam shafts; the JH 61 and JDJ 74 cu.in. machines were expensive and fast. More prosaically, but more importantly, the ordinary J model gained a front brake and a larger oil pump. In the same year, the model C was released, which survived into the next season as the model CK. This single cylinder side-valve machine was not a hit with the dealers and certainly not with the buying public. They overheated and looked odd. The R series of long stroke 45 cu.in. twins, didn't offer enough speed. In this period of the company's history, a lack of direction can be detected, and in the case of these two series, a kind of technical confusion. The single cylinder machines were given the same frame as the twins, which made them too heavy. The twin, with what was a single cylinder clutch and gearbox, was consequently unreliable. This slightly muddled desire to keep costs down by using the same frame and components on different machines, conflicted with H-D's wish to challenge the popular 101 Scout from Indian, a small twin which was selling very well. The company tried to rectify some of the faults as the murmurs of discontent swelled, with larger carburetors, fuel and oil tanks, but it was too late.

With the same kind of uncertainty, the company shot itself in the foot even when it came to its core business, the big twin. The 74 cu.in. VL was a side-valve machine produced in 1929 to replace the long-running J series. It was incredibly heavy, and the

Harley-Davidson

30.50C "BABY HARLEY" 1929

Unpopular at home, the "Baby Harley" sold well abroad, especially in Japan, where it was available until 1937 (as opposed to 1934 in the States).

Designations	C, CM
Engine	side-valve single
Bore & stroke	3$\frac{3}{32}$ × 4 in.
Displacement	30.50 cu.in.
Suspension	springer front forks
BHP	10
Top speed	approx. 60 mph

BELOW: The 61 cu. in. V-twin was the mainstay of the company when sales had plummeted in 1921. A front brake wasn't considered necessary until 1927.

power rating was no better than the two cam JH model. The flywheels were very small in an attempt to improve acceleration: the result, naturally, was lack of torque. The side-valve configuration was chosen partly because of the success of Indian with side-valve machines: once again, arguably a case of keeping your eye on the opposition, not the ball. Many law cnforcement agencies canceled their orders when the rumors of underperformance became too loud, and some dealers actually defected to Indian or Excelsior. Harley-Davidson appeared to have made a serious mistake. The company replaced the small flywheels, which meant providing a larger crankcase, and while they were about it, they redesigned the cams. Finally, the bike needed a new frame. It all cost a lot of money, a lot of sales, and a lot of goodwill. Harley-Davidson had the dealership network, the sales, and ultimately the product to brush aside

RIGHT: An example from the last year for the Sixty One J pocket valve twin, 1929. The 61 cu. in. Harley-Davidson would storm back seven years later with the knucklehead.

OPPOSITE, ABOVE: Photographed back in 1988, it is to be hoped that this beautiful machine is still in good order today. In 1929, Harley-Davidson had 45, 61, and 74 cu. in. V-twins on offer, and the twin cam race-derived 74 cu. in. special.

these setbacks where others would have faltered. On the positive side, the side valve 45 V-twin would prove to be the first of a marvelous series of machines which would be in production for the next 24 years.

Several design improvements through the roller coaster twenties should be highlighted: drop-forged steel frame fittings, improved lubrication systems (though the VL still had a total loss system) metallurgical refinements, a new single coil ignition system, an overall widening of customer choice. In addition, Harley-Davidson came to dominate the AMA (American Motorcycle Association), the organization which represented motorcyclists' interests, when Indian refused to increase its subsidy in 1928, distracted by diversification away from motorcycles.

Fortunately, 1929 turned out to be a good year for the industry as a whole, with output at 31,000 machines, 21,000 of which were Harley-Davidsons. But protectionism was becoming popular in Europe; and the world economic slump would be devastating.

Harley-Davidson

FORTY-FIVE D 1929

A mainstay of the Harley-Davidson stable, this series of 45s was produced between 1929 and 52.

Designations	D, DL, DLD, R, RL, RLD, W, WL, WLD, WLDR, WLA, WLAC
Engine	side-valve V-twin
Bore & stroke	2¾ × 3^{13}⁄16 in.
Displacement	45 cu.in.
Suspension	springer front forks
BHP	20
Top speed	55-65 mph

CHAPTER FOUR

THE DEPRESSION

We may be able to keep you on until the Spring

HARLEY-DAVIDSON

"We may be able to keep you on until the spring" (William A. Davidson)

Black Tuesday, October 29, 1929, Wall Street; not the first time, and not the last, that the world was reminded just what real wealth is. Real wealth is work, manufacturing, the creation of goods from raw materials, (like Harley-Davidson) and not stock market margins. The devastation caused by that lapse of memory was massive. 5000 banks failed and ultimately 30 percent of the US working population lost their jobs.

Ironically, 1930 was a fairly good year for Harley-Davidson. Single cylinder sales slipped; most sales of the single cylinder machines were abroad. The twins sold just as many as in the previous year: all that excitement on Wall Street, brokers leaping out of windows, Carnegie's representative's dramatic but forlorn attempt to shore up the market with the words "I buy steel", perhaps it was all just irrelevant. Some people began to feel that President Hoover may have done enough to prevent any long-lasting damage. The optimism was illusory, of course. In November 1930 those workers who could be kept on at the Harley-Davidson factory took a 10 percent pay cut. Production in 1931 was more or less halved. Revenue in 1932 was a third of what it has been in 1930.

There is no single reason why Harley-Davidson survived the disaster where others failed, soon out-selling Indian two to one, and watching the third big player, Excelsior, disappear. In fact, it was more or less a question of doing what was done in the previous decade, but doing it better and harder. Harley-Davidson advertising in the 1930s was colorful and confident; sales abroad were doggedly pursued and became even more vital as the domestic market inexorably shrank. Accessories were also marketed even more vigorously. The utility market was critical to survival, and over 3000 police departments were on H-Ds in 1930.

The possibility of shutting the factory doors for good was very real in 1932, but the second generation of Harleys and Davidsons – William J. Harley, William H., (who would become president in 1942) Allan, Gordon and Walter C. Davidson – were not going to give up their birthright without a struggle. The shortcomings of the 1929 model range would eventually be put right. The 45s were not radically altered until 1936, once the engine had been redesigned (and not surprisingly, until that momentous year, the decade was not one of technical innovation across the range). If slow, and with suspect transmission, they at least had the advantage of the characteristic oversized cooling fins on the cylinder heads, which allowed for problem-free idling. Their war service ensured that they became some of the best-loved Harley-Davidsons of all, despite the obvious attractions of the big twins.

PREVIOUS PAGES: In many ways it is miraculous that Harley-Davidson were producing machines like this magnificent 1939 knucklehead EL by the end of that dread decade. The survival of the company is a tribute to ingenuity, business *sang froid* and sheer hard graft.

OPPOSITE: 74 cu. in. side valve twin, in production from 1930 to 1936, this a VL. Olive drab was out by 1933, and art deco tank graphics were in.

HARLEY-DAVIDSON

In 1932 the 45 cu.in. "Servi-Car" was introduced. This machine had a chain-driven car-type back axle, and a variety of bodies could be attached for commercial use. It is an interesting example of Uncle Sam borrowing ideas from Japan and the Far East, rather than the more usual reversal of roles which would be complained of in years to come. The rickshaw-type machine had been produced in the East for some ten years by this time. The low compression three-wheelers were used not just for deliveries but also by traffic cops. The officer would cruise past the parked cars and mark the rear tire with a chalk stick. When he came back to find you had overstayed your welcome, a citation would result. The Servi-Car was also used by garages to tow vehicles. The rear wheels were 3ft. 6in. apart, which made it easier for the "non-rider" to follow the ruts made by cars in snow or mud. The 21 and 30.5 cu.in. single cylinders weren't all bad news: the Ricardo removeable heads made for ease of maintenance, as did larger brakes and tires.

After its inauspicious start, the 74 cu.in. VL was improved; and once again, not everything was bad. Quick-release wheels were a boon, and on a less technical note, the gas tanks of 1932 have some of the loveliest Art Deco paint ever seen on a motorcycle. Allied to the new lower riding position which would become an H-D hallmark,

BELOW: The Servi-Car was originally introduced for use by garages for pickup and delivery of cars, but it soon found a more general utility market.

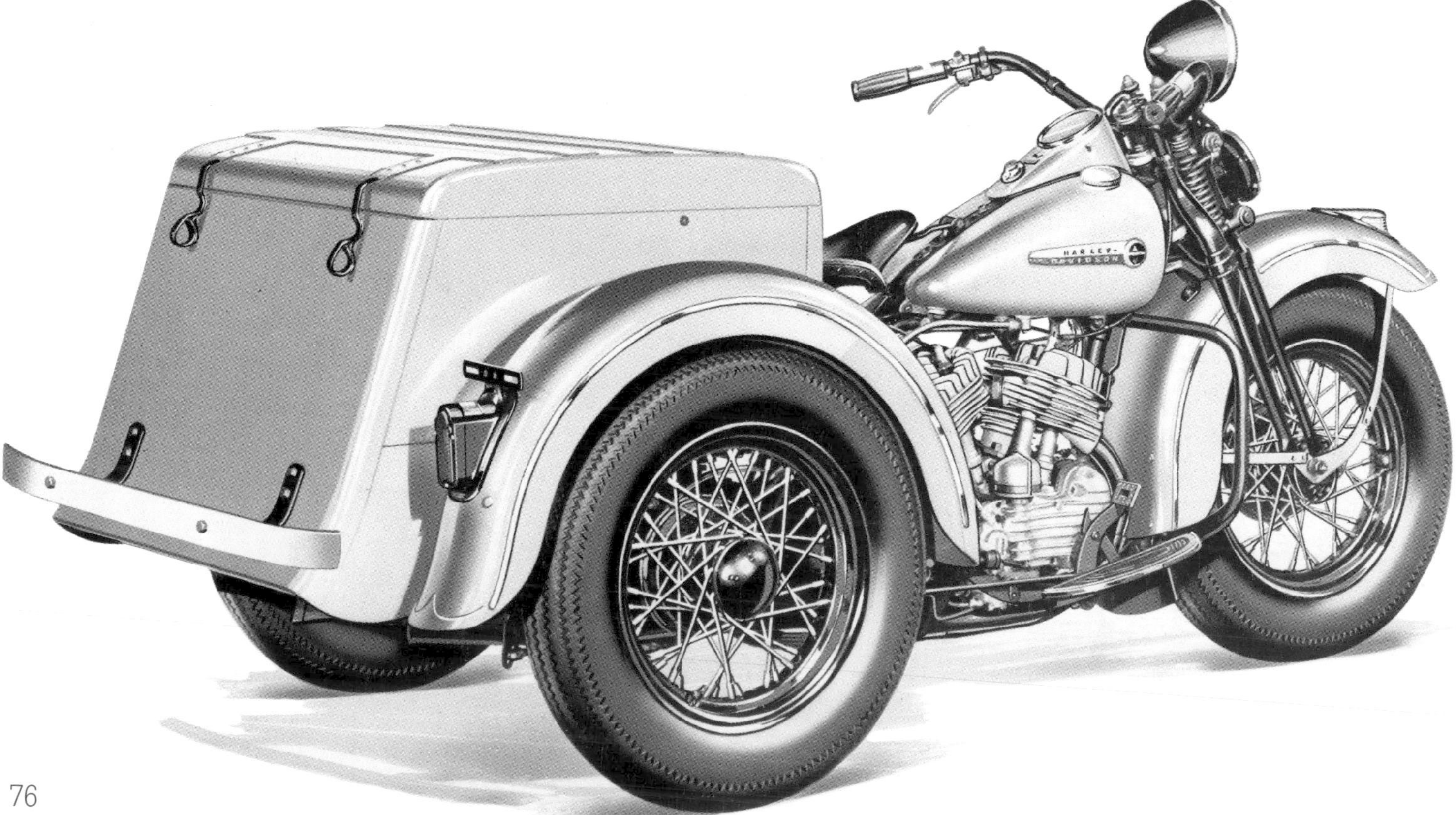

ABOVE AND LEFT: The Servi-Car would be around for a long time. Introduced in 1932, this example (top) was actually built in the mid-1960s, and the police version (left) in 1967. By then, however, it had acquired an electric starter.

they looked the part. Just as Henry Ford had flooded the market earlier with cut-price cars because of overproduction (and consequently was making substantial losses by 1928), so the police model VL was offered direct to the public, cutting out the hard-pressed dealers altogether, at a knockdown price that barely covered manufacturing costs. The uneasy relationship with Indian, whereby agreements on pricing structure had been hammered out, now went to the wall, as would, eventually, the Indian company, but not for some time yet. When the going got tough some dealers defected to Indian, other simply gave up.

The two companies carved up the remaining domestic market roughly equally, but Harley-Davidson were selling twice as many machines because of exports. South America, Britain, Japan, and Scandinavia were keeping the company alive. The sales numbers were tiny in comparison with the golden age of the early 1920s, but were enough. The singles were not even listed for sale stateside from 1934, but continued to be exported. In 1936, an 80 cu.in. side-valve twin was introduced, simply a bored out VL 74. But that wasn't the big news that year.

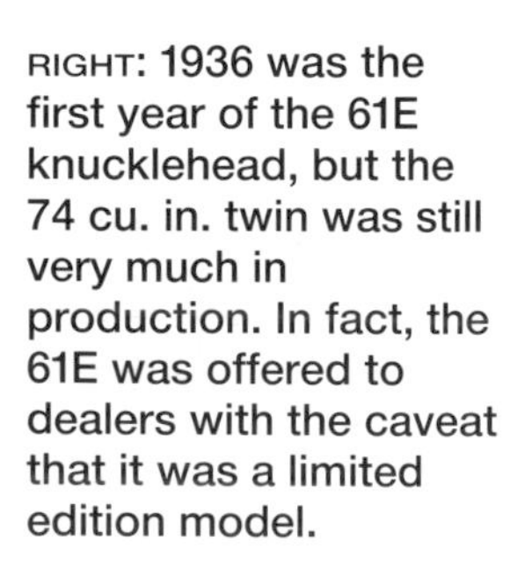

RIGHT: 1936 was the first year of the 61E knucklehead, but the 74 cu. in. twin was still very much in production. In fact, the 61E was offered to dealers with the caveat that it was a limited edition model.

ABOVE RIGHT: Compare the frame of the 74 cu. in. VL with the double loop frame of the knucklehead on page 80. The teardrop tank will become shorter and more rounded.

Harley-Davidson

74 VL TWIN 1931

74s had been around since 1922, but 1930 saw the introduction of the side-valve twin engine. The new motorcycle had an inauspicious start when early machines had to have their engines completely revamped due to lack of power.

Designations	V, VL, VS (sidecar), VC (Package Truck)
Engine	'Flathead' side-valve twin
Bore & stroke	$3\frac{7}{16} \times 4$ in.
Displacement	74 cu.in.
Suspension	springer front forks
Tires	balloon 27 x 4.00
Top speed	approx. 80 mph

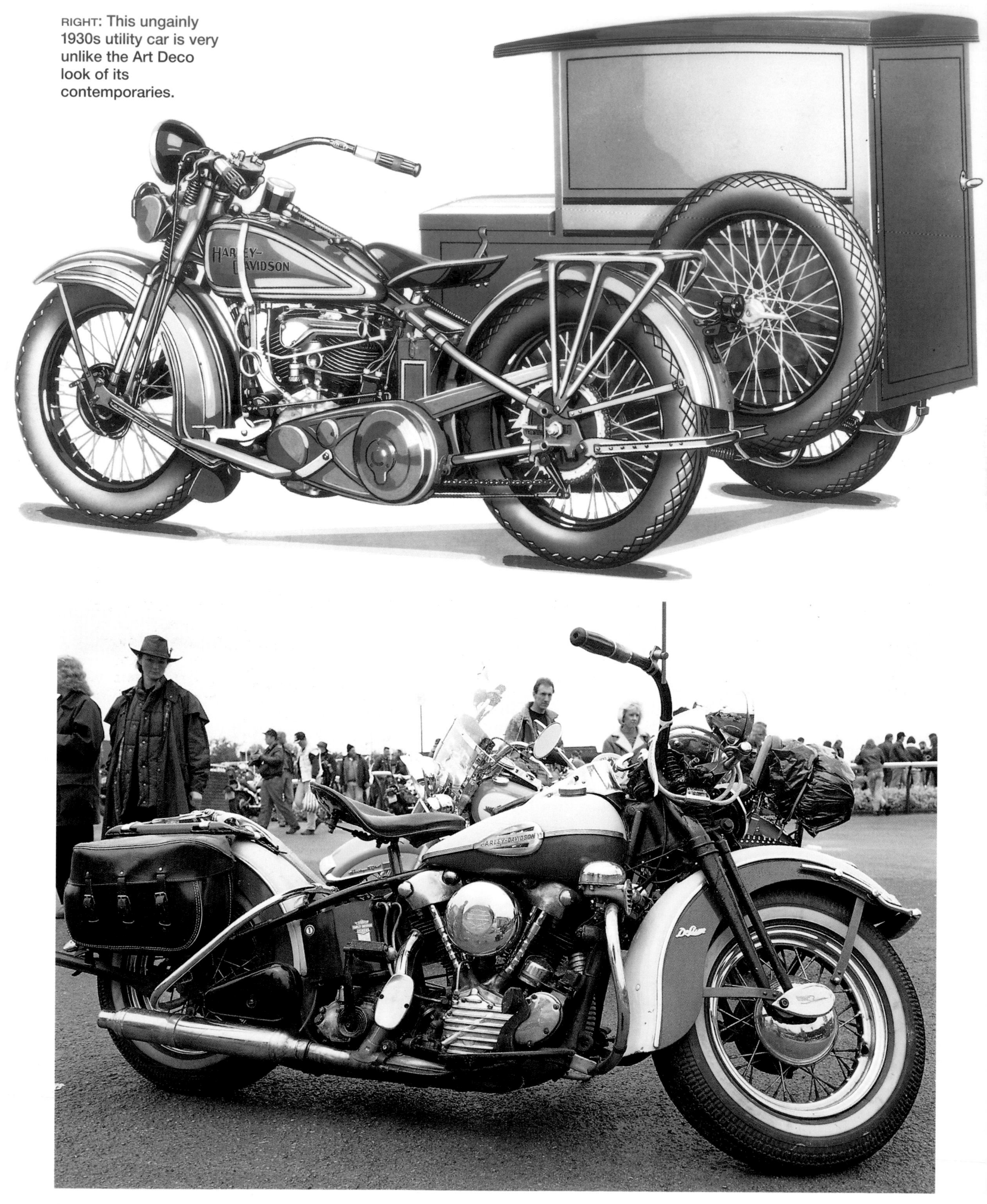

RIGHT: This ungainly 1930s utility car is very unlike the Art Deco look of its contemporaries.

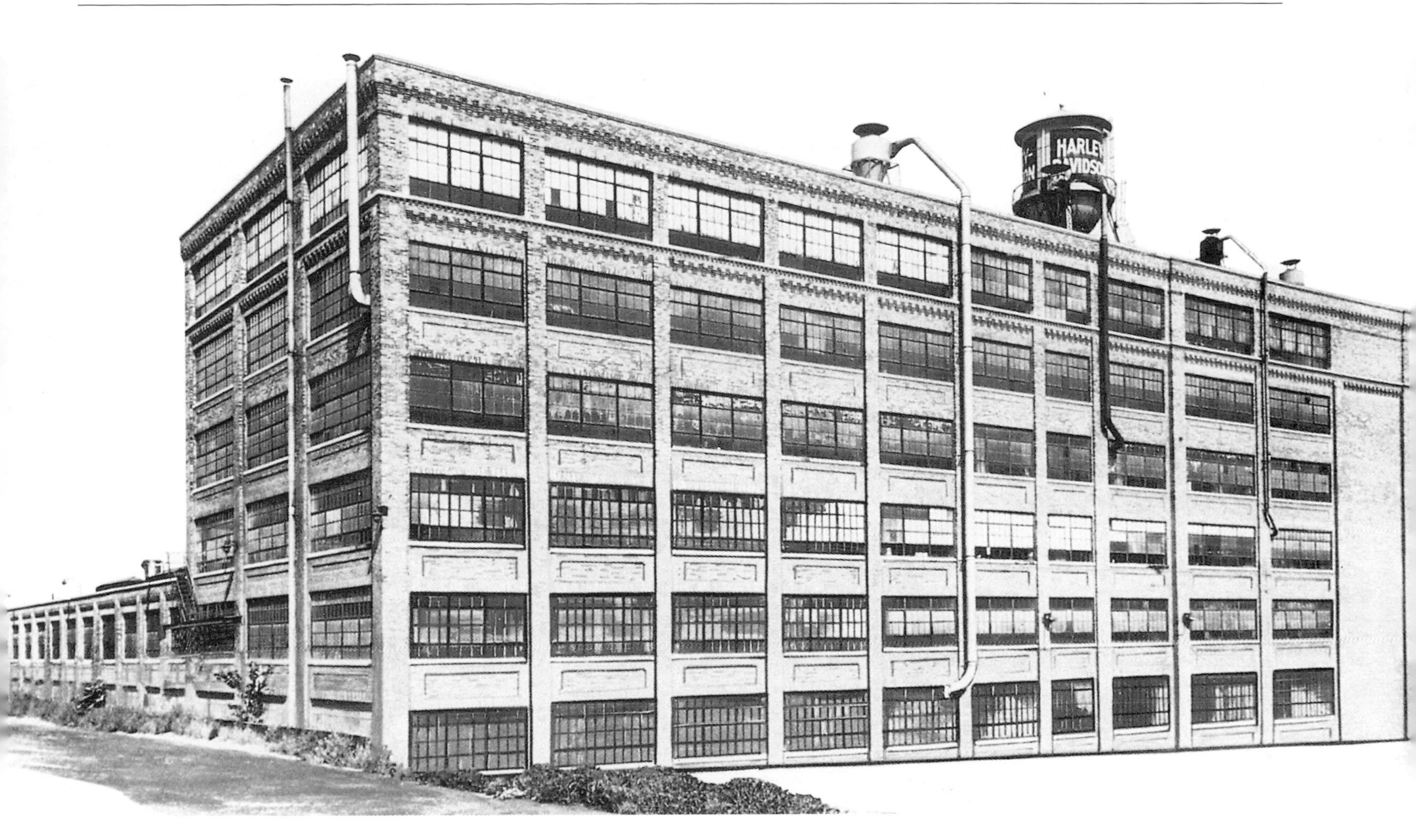

It could be argued that the bedrock of the Harley-Davidson company as we know it today was set down in 1936.

It was in that year that the 61E was introduced, which would evolve through EL, F and FL models right up to 1947. First, why was the engine nicknamed "Knucklehead"? Sit on the machine and look down to your right. The lumps of the rocker box you see below you look (more or less) like the protruding knuckles of a fist. A single camshaft's four lobes lead to pushrods up through tubes to the heads. The carb is in the middle of the V, along with the intake ports, and the exhaust pipes out wide. To the front and right of the front pushrods is the ignition timer, with the generator (6v) below the front cylinder. The total loss oil system, which was exactly what it says, was abandoned in favor of a system whereby fluctuations in crankcase pressure were exploited to pull oil back from the heads into the crankcase. It wasn't a truly revolutionary system, and it meant that seals had to be perfect, which they weren't, but it *felt* revolutionary and was an excellent selling point for the hard-pressed dealers. The engine hung in a double tube cradle, which in retro

ABOVE: **In 1936, just under a quarter of Harley-Davidson output from the Juneau Avenue factory was of the new 61E.**

LEFT: **It's a knucklehead, but with a slightly more up-to-date S&S carb and filter.**

OPPOSITE, BELOW: **The unequal length push rods inside the angled tubes of the ohv knucklehead make it identifiable from a mile away. The ignition timer is forward of the front push rods.**

Harley-Davidson

61E "KNUCKLEHEAD" 1936

Available until 1947, the "Knucklehead" engine was the precursor of today's Harley-Davidson engines.

Designations	E, EL, F, FL
Engine	ohv V-twin
Bore & stroke	3⅝₁₆ × 3½ in.
Displacement	61 cu.in.
Suspension	leading link front forks
BHP	60
Top speed	approx. 90 mph

JOKER

ABOVE: Front suspension on a 45 cu. in. 1930s Harley-Davidson. Springer forks were the order of the day from 1907 until 1949.

RIGHT: 1940 61EL ex-police motorcycle. The "Sentinels of Safety" as the Harley-Davidson advertising copy called them, were a very important part of sales. The semicircular footboards were new for that year.

spect seems such an obvious advance on the old, bicycle-like single tube, which was apparently inadequate for holding such a large lump of metal. The frame itself was still a diamond shape bicycle-type, with a down-tube from the seat. It would prove to be too light later, and would be strengthened. The valves leaked, so larger versions of the distinctive rocker covers were used on 1938 examples.

Secondly, how fast was it? Fast enough at around 90 mph. Perhaps more importantly, the whole package looked just fine, (and still does today) from the finned barrels to the foot boards, teardrop tank and oil damped, sprung saddle; there was no rear suspension yet. The uprated EL version offered higher compression, which naturally didn't satisfy the speedsters for ever, and the ohv 61 would become 74 F (FL and FS for sidecar) in 1941, when the old flathead 74, having grown to 80 cu.in. was dropped as uneconomic competition for the more modern design.

This is the first machine from the company that you only need to glance at for half a second, through the thickest California coastal fog (though you won't see many around today), to know instantly that it is a Harley-Davidson. The wraparound oil tank, the teardrop gas tank, the rocker covers, the riding position itself, even the fancy new instrument panel with integrated speedometer, all scream Harley. The machine wasn't cheap, but just enough were sold to justify the tooling costs. In the conservative spirit of Works Manager and Vice-President William A. Davidson, who died on April 21st

Blue Knights

1937, nothing radical would happen to the design for the next five years; and postwar demand would keep the machines selling. Today, a 61E must surely be one of the most desirable machines for the H-D fan, but it won't come cheap. One telling fact about H-D history, and in fact a reminder of just how different the motorcycle industry as a whole was back then, is that it is possible to, for example, use the next generation of cylinders – that is, a 1948 panhead – on a knucklehead engine, if you have the patience and skill. You will need three panhead cylinders, one as a template and one of the bolt holes on the head gasket will be out of line, but the mere fact that the operation is possible at all points to the steady evolution of Harley-Davidson machines through the decades, and the implication that machines were supposed to last over many years and be restored or adapted by their owners or professional workshops. Imagine trying to shoehorn engineering back and forth in this way between different generations, even different model years, of motorcycles today. Come to think of it, imagine attempting *any* kind of major surgery on, say, even a machine as old as the six cylinder CBX1000 from Honda. One look at that massive block is enough to tell most people "Don't mess with me," and as for contemporary black box, computer-controlled fuel injection aluminum box section multi-valve liquid-cooled superbikes, forget it.

The great racer Joe Petrali (much more on him in the 'Competition' chapter) and Hank Syvertsen from the racing department were behind the new design of the 61E. Joe Petrali took a 61 to Daytona in 1937 and

BELOW: **1939 WLD 45 cu. in. factory racer, with aluminum heads. The DLDR was produced as a speed version of the old 45 at the end of the 1930s for Class C competition, but it couldn't challenge Indian's Sport Scout.**

claimed the unsupercharged world record at 136.83 mph. Police Officer Fred Hamm performed an astounding feat of endurance in the same year at what is now the Edwards Airforce Base in California, covering 1825 miles in 24 hours, with an average speed of 76.02 mph. Astounding? Yes, the previous 24-hour record had been held by a team of four Frenchmen: Fred rode alone.

It will come as no surprise to Harley-Davidson lovers that H-D helped establish the Japanese motorcycle industry. As has already been mentioned, Japan had been an important export market from the mid-1920s. The H-D Motorcycle Sales Company of Japan had been established in 1924 under the guidance of the remarkable Alfred Rich Child, a sales prodigy if ever there was one. In 1929 the yen collapsed, which threatened the complex, but profitable ex-

ABOVE: Coil ignition was a problem in competition as the condensers tended to burn out. In 1941 the factory would produce the WLR, with a refined engine and magneto ignition.

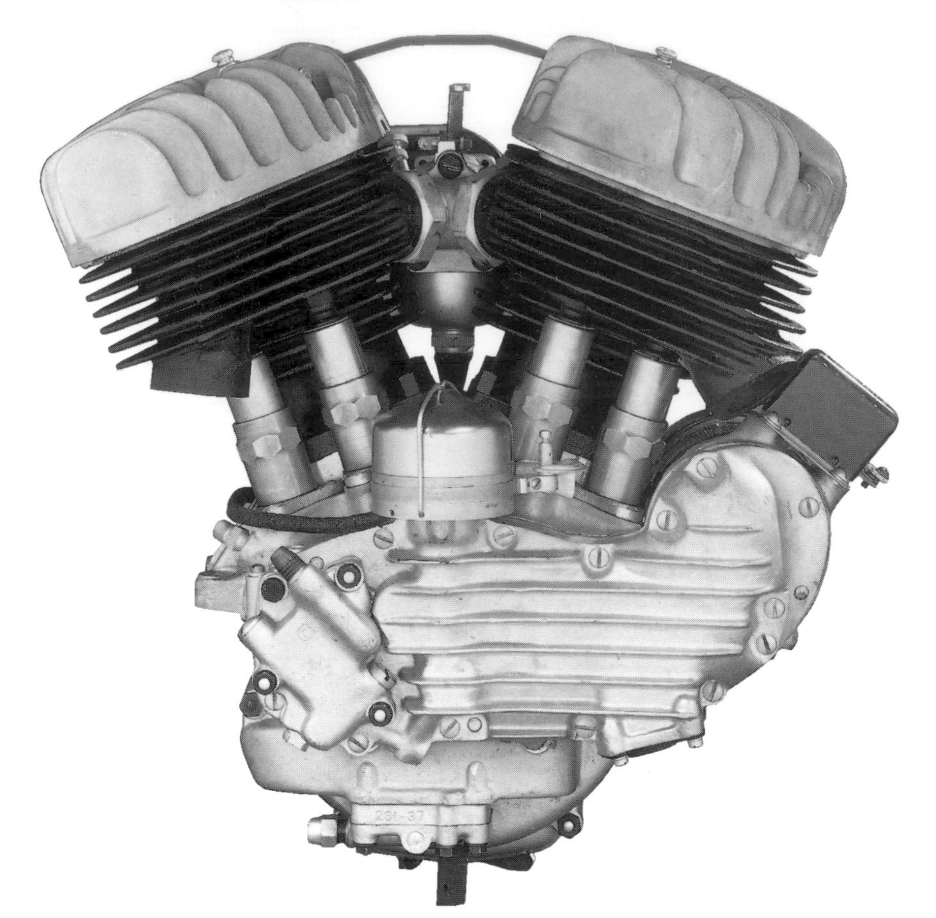

ABOVE: 1940 45 cu. in. engine, with alloy heads.

BELOW: Completely original 1934 45, owned by Tom Payne.

OPPOSITE: The springer front forks of a 1940 VL. There's no face like chrome.

port dealership network that had been established. Child succeeded in persuading the H-D management to license the Sankyo company to produce machines on their home soil. It must have been quite a sales pitch, but it was helped by the worldwide depression. By 1935, the Shinagawa factory was capable of producing complete machines from H-D blueprints. The old side-valve machines, with lower top speed, but more torque at low speeds were preferred to the new 61E, which displayed all of its early teething troubles on a 400 mile test run in Japan by Alfred's son Richard. As Japanese militarism took a firmer hold, the contract was dissolved, but the side-valve UL model continued to be manufactured as the "Rikuo" throughout the war. The original VL became, under instruction from the Japanese government, the Type 97 Military Model, and nearly 19,000 were built, mostly for sidecar work. This was a truly fascinating interlude in H-D history, and the complexity of the various agreements and the uneasy feelings of the parent company concerning its oriental offshoot as Pearl Harbor approached, deserve a book in themselves. Let's just say that Harley-Davidson showed Honda, Kawasaki, Yamaha and Suzuki how to do it. It's not true, but it's easier to follow.

CHAPTER FIVE

WINNING THE PEACE

The Second Golden Age of Motorcycling

GLAD

While tens of thousands of WLA 45s were advancing on Berlin (from east and west) civilian production was cut to a dribble of utility vehicles, mostly for the police, and for those who could persuade the authorities that a Harley-Davidson was essential to their own personal war effort. Competition was scaled down, but the company tried to keep things ticking over through organized club events. Plant tours, which had been a feature for many years, were stopped even before US entry into the war, in 1941. Aluminum for pistons was difficult to acquire, and oil was sold in glass bottles to conserve metal. The American birthright – cheap and plentiful gas – was temporarily suspended. Because the factory was running practically beyond capacity through the war years in order to supply the military, it was not in such bad shape when the victors finally came home. Despite material shortages, updated versions of the 1941 models were ready for 1947. The most important new feature was the hydraulic shock absorber, alongside a new taillight design and a little more chrome. The accessories catalog was a real Aladdin's cave, featuring in particular a rather natty black leather jacket with zippered sleeves, derivatives of which are now worn by ten million people who have never been so much as a pillion passenger on a Honda 90.

One new machine appeared, which was unlike earlier Harleys: the two-stroke S-125. The three-speed lightweight with its rigid frame and Lilliputian 3 bhp was based upon the German DKW RT 125. As part of war reparations, the British – BSA Bantam – the Japanese and the Italians (um, war reparations?) also took the design and exploited it, some more effectively than others. This machine would grow up into the Tele-Glide (telescopic forks) get more ccs, become the Hummer in the 1960s, then the 165cc "Super Ten" and was the first fruit of a flirtation by the company with lightweight machines that would never really become a marriage, except under AMF management. It should not be underestimated, however, as more than 100,000 were sold.

1948 saw a record number of Harley-Davidsons produced, with aluminum heads on the 61 and 74 cu.in. engines, together with the very ritzy hydraulic valve lifters, (to be found in, for example, Alfa Romeos, but not for another year in the products from GM), and one-piece, chromed rocker covers would give rise to the nickname "panhead". The record production figures were helped by the opening of the new 260,000 square feet machine shop that year on Capitol Drive. The covers were secured with a metal ring and a series of bolts. If you took it off, with a little imagination it might remind you of a baking or frying pan. (More obvious than the origins of the name knucklehead, anyway.) The changes were introduced to improve oil flow and consumption. The oil pump was larger and oil lines were neatly tucked away inside. It worked. Foot clutch

PREVIOUS PAGES: **A late 1950s M-165 single cylinder two-stroke. Harley-Davidson would make constant attempts to compete in the lightweight and middleweight markets over the next three decades, but it would always be the big V-twins which dominated production.**

RIGHT: **Custom built 1956 74 cu. in. FLH panhead. The heads are topped by covers held in place by a metal ring and bolts – hence the nickname for the new engine. In 1955, the bottom end of the panhead was improved, with stronger main bearings.**

Harley-Davidson
MOTOR
HARLEY DAVIDSON
CYCLES
MADE IN U.S.A.
WAGNER

Harley-Davidson

S-125 1947

Harley-Davidson's first new postwar model came as something of a surprise.

Designations	M-125, S, ST
Engine	single 2-stroke
Bore & stroke	2 1/16 × 2 9/32 in.
Displacement	7.6 cu.in.
Compression ratio	6.6:1
BHP	3
Top speed	50 mph

and hand shift was still the order of the day.

In 1949 there was another major development with the introduction of telescopic forks. Farewell to Bill Harley's trusty springer forks that had been such a great idea so long ago. The innovation was important enough to warrant a model name; this was something new for Harley-Davidson – before then all machines had letters, numbers or nicknames. The Hydra-Glide was a Sumo, with 5.00 × 16 in. tires, a much larger front drum brake, rigid rear suspension of course, with no-nonsense (dare we say

Harley-Davidson

MODEL B HUMMER 1959

A spin-off from the 125cc DKW clone, the home-grown single cylinder machine would quickly give way to the new Aermacchi/ Harley-Davidson lightweights.

Designations	n/a
Engine	2-stroke single cylinder
Bore & stroke	2 1/16 × 2 9/32 in.
Displacement	7.6 cu. in. (125 cc)
Compression ratio	6.6:1
BHP	3
Top speed	60 mph

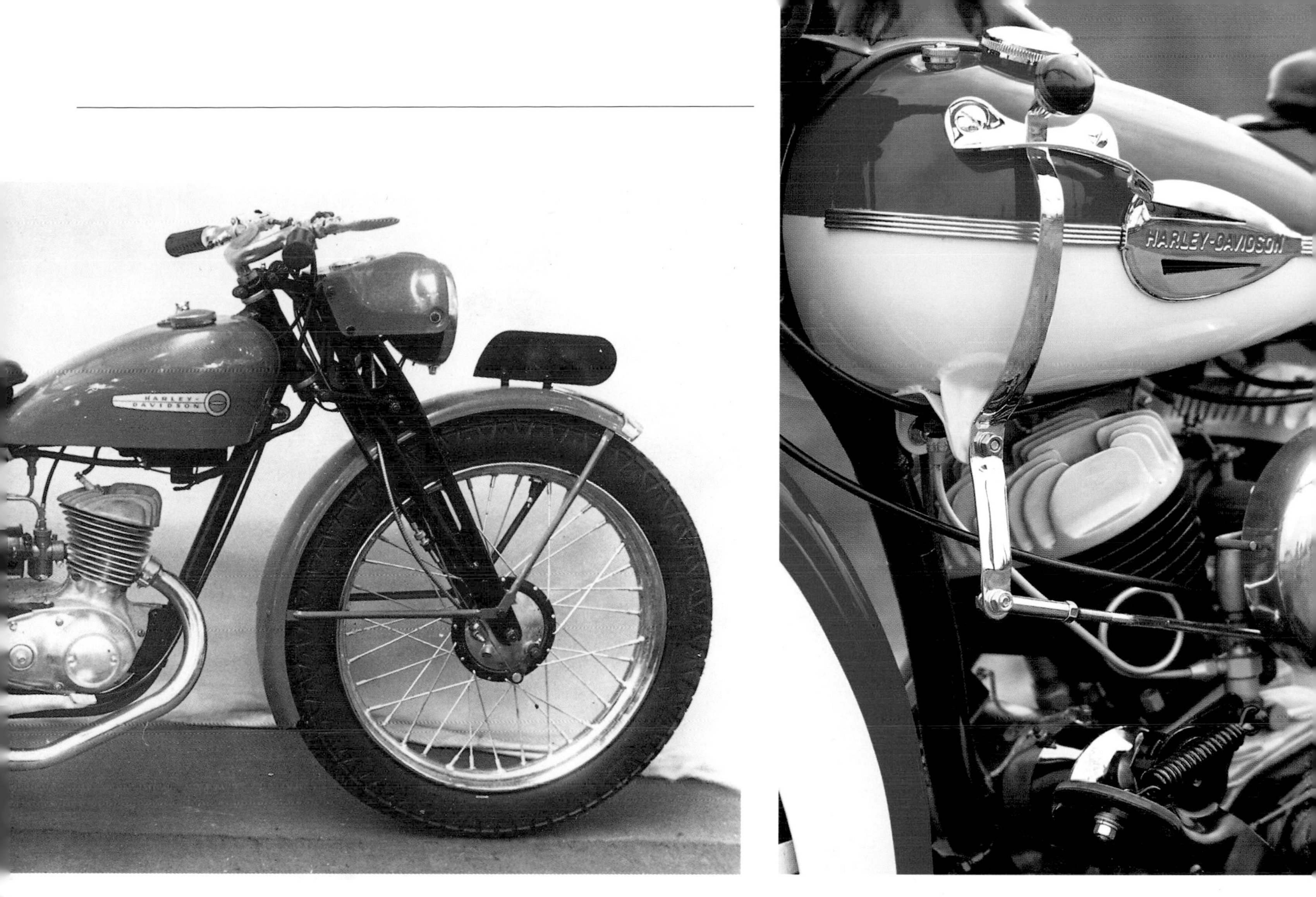

ABOVE LEFT: A 125 cc single cylinder Harley-Davidson on display at the Drussels motorcycle show in 1950. The importance of overseas markets – particularly for some of the lightweight H-D machines – cannot be overestimated in the company's unending struggle for financial security.

ABOVE: This 1946 flathead 45 WL engine has been completely restored by owner Phil Argersinger.

LEFT: The 125 cc Hummer, produced from 1947 to 1953. It weighed 170 lbs, and offered the young rider something like 90 miles to the gallon.

ABOVE AND OPPOSITE:
1949 panhead Hydra-Glide. The ohv 61 and 74 engines featured hydraulic valve lifters and aluminum heads. The panhead would be the bedrock of production for the next 20 years.

Indian-looking) fenders and roly poly covers over the fork tubes. The machine wasn't just conjured up overnight: several prototypes had been designed and rejected since before the war. Rubber-mounted bars were introduced, along with a more comfortable latex-filled saddle. Corrosion protection was also improved. For 1950, as befits the start of arguably the United States' finest decade, 10 hp was added by various means.

The 1950s were not Harley's finest hour, but Harley-Davidson motorcycles are loved by Europeans – and some Americans – for the same reasons that 1950s America is regarded with nostalgia. For solidity, for being aspirational, for expressing a kind of optimism by their very existence. Freedom, individuality, and sheer bulk. Despite the various trials the company would undergo in the next two decades, that symbolism was never lost. Love of Harley-Davidsons today is intimately connected with American postwar cultural dominance.

The FL Panhead was the basis for nearly 20 years of production, and in the early 1950s the design was tweaked constantly. In 1951 the engine could produce 55 bhp; in 1952 a foot gear change was introduced, along with the 45 cu.in. K model, and the KH 55 cu.in. two years on; and in 1953 you got a special airhorn amongst other goodies produced for the Jubilee: "50 years – American made."

Two years previously, the company had argued for an increase in taxes on imported machines, with no result. The British motorcycle invasion was on. British vertical twins wiped the floor with the slow, if technically forward-looking four-speed K models, and the company tried to diversify into lawn mowers, scooters and other, more irrelevant

Harley-Davidson

74FL "HYDRA-GLIDE" 1952

The "Hydra-Glide" was the first Harley to have a model name as opposed to a letter or number, a change that came with the introduction of telescopic forks in 1949. Developed using the "Panhead" motor, the "Hydra-Glide" evolved into the "Duo-Glide" in 1958 and the 'Electra-Glide' in 1965.

Designations	n/a
Engine	ohv V-twin
Bore & stroke	3.43 × 3.96 in.
Displacement	74 cu.in.
Suspension	telescopic forks
BHP	55
Top speed	100 mph (claimed)

HARLEY
DAVIDSON

LEFT: A lovely example of an FL 1948 panhead, owned by Essex Motorsports, Chester, CT. That year also saw the opening of the new plant on Capitol Drive. It was a watershed year following the "artificial" economic situation of wartime production. The new engine, the new equipment options and the new plant all trumpeted confidence.

BELOW: In many ways the Model K was the forerunner of the Sportster. Lefthand clutch, right foot gear shift; telescopic tubes at the front, swing arm at the back.

machinery. In 1949, 24,000 machines were sold; in 1955 just 9500. Profits were still made, but more as a result of the postwar boom in the entire industry rather than through astute marketing on the part of Harley-Davidson. The trusty 61 was dropped in favor of 74 cu.in.

"How does Elvis rate cover position in *The Enthusiast*? He is a Harley-Davidson rider . . . and at present rides the 1956 KH. It is a red and white model and is his favorite." The company had not forgotten the importance of advertising: they just didn't have the middleweight muscle to challenge AJS and Matchless, Norton and Triumph. Nor did Indian. Their brittle Arrow and Scout vertical twins would finally be the death of Harley-Davidson's only remaining domestic competitor. Ironically, the big Indian V-twins were just about as good as ever, but the seductive sight of all that middleweight money flowing across the Atlantic (and gratefully received by what was in effect a bankrupt nation) had proved too much.

Why didn't H-D's K series seriously challenge the overseas competition? It is too easy to say that the company was just too slow to tool up after the war and invest in new designs. The inherent conservatism of the company, with its strong family ties, had seen it through the economic minefield of the 1930s, and who can say that the same

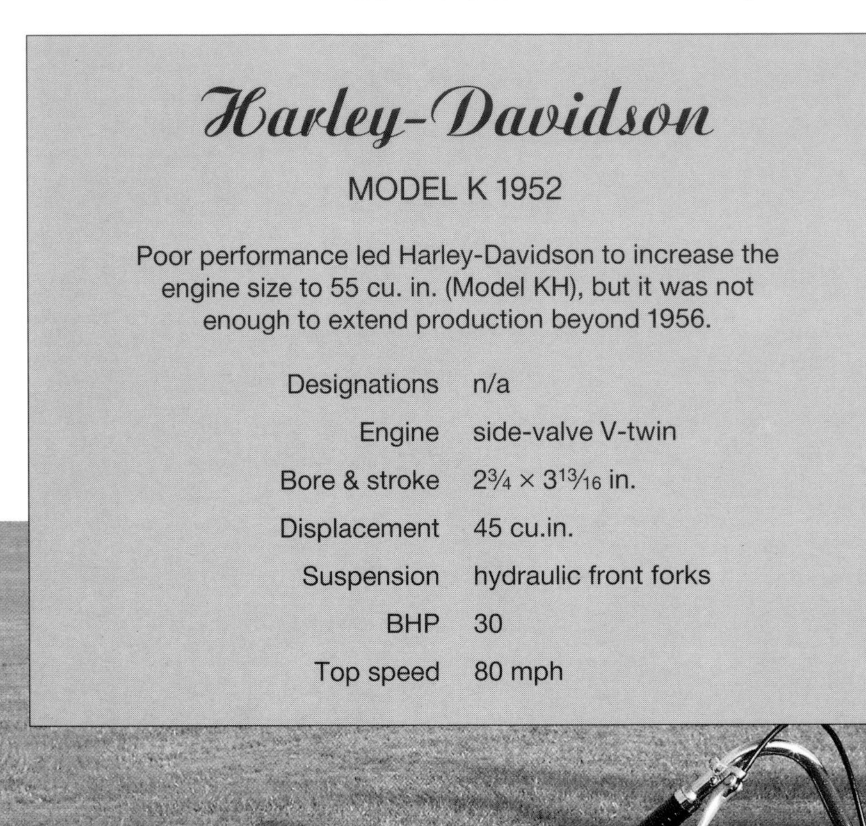

Harley-Davidson

MODEL K 1952

Poor performance led Harley-Davidson to increase the engine size to 55 cu. in. (Model KH), but it was not enough to extend production beyond 1956.

Designations	n/a
Engine	side-valve V-twin
Bore & stroke	$2\frac{3}{4} \times 3\frac{13}{16}$ in.
Displacement	45 cu.in.
Suspension	hydraulic front forks
BHP	30
Top speed	80 mph

LEFT: The K grew up into the 55 cu. in. (or more accurately 54) KH, to compensate for the lack of power. The valves were bigger and the clutch was new.

BELOW: The bore remained the same at 2¾ in. but the stroke was lengthened to 4$\frac{9}{16}$ in. The unit construction, with crankcase and gearbox all of a piece, was new for H-D.

ABOVE: Fifty years between the machines – 1902 to 1952 – and a new Harley-Davidson management generation. From left to right: John Harley, product engineer; Walter C. Davidson, secretary; William H. Davidson, president; Gordon Davidson, vice-president; William J. Harley, treasurer and chief engineer.

reluctance to diversify away from the big twins with any real conviction did not save the company from following the same dusty road to death as Indian? No-one could know that the motorcycle market would be ten times the size it had been in 1950 by the end of the decade. One great advantage that the British manufacturers held was cheap labor; Harley-Davidson were obliged to negotiate with the United Auto Workers, and disruption at the plant was not uncommon in the 1950s and 1960s. Collective bargaining is one of the greatest inventions since the combustion engine, though the H-D management of the time would not have agreed, and it did not make for a level playing field.

One aspect of the H-D story which cannot be neglected starts around about here, in 1954. *The Wild One*, starring Marlon Brando (riding a nice clean Triumph Speed Twin, as everyone knows) Lee Marvin and Mary Murphy, was released. It was loosely based on a fight in 1947 at Hollister, California between bikers and some outraged townsfolk. It was a fairly big punch-up, involving 500 lawmen, and made the papers in a big way, including *Life* magazine. It was the first movie to portray bikers and, as has been mentioned before, Harley-Davidson had always been acutely conscious of the image of motorcycling, having made strenuous efforts through the AMA to keep it clean. In one sense the "full-dresser" Harley was originally part of that conservative outlook. The company certainly didn't take to the new craze of chopping their machines. But there just seems to be an immutable law that says if a company pares its products down, people will add bits; if it supplies full fairings and big, sensible tanks, people will strip them off. The Harley-Davidson was already, and had been for some time, far more than just a means of transport. As an expression of *un art de vivre*, it was always going to get into trouble, particularly as it was noisy, dirty and dangerous.

The double-edged sword of the outlaw connection has always taxed H-D top brass. In the 1970s they ran an ad showing Hells Angels, or something very like them, with a line expressing the company's reluctance to produce inferior goods for such a dangerous crew. The company was criticized for it, unsurprisingly. The only thing that can be said about the outlaw connection without offending the huge majority of law-abiding H-D riders, or the company, or the members of the various chapters, is that there is a supreme irony in the long-standing relationship between one of the oldest, conservative companies in corporate America and

LEFT: It's a free country . . .

BELOW: 1953, director Laslo Benedek, producer Stanley Kramer, *The Wild One*. The film actually had two other titles, *Cyclists Raid* and *Hot Blood*. As everyone knows, Marlon did not ride one of Milwaukee's finest, but bad boy Lee Marvin did.

Harley-Davidson

SPORTSTER XL 1957

The longest Harley-Davidson production run began with the XL in 1957.

Designations	n/a
Engine	ohv V-twin
Bore & stroke	3 × 3.81 in.
Displacement	54 cu. in.
Suspension	telescopic forks, swing-arm rear
BHP	40
Top speed	90 mph (claimed)

some of its quasi-anarchic customers.

The 1950s saw a division of the company's efforts and its customer base which is still in force, although sometimes the machines become very close, almost interchangeable. The division is, of course, between Glides and Sportsters. The difference, to put it crudely, is between touring and speed, between comfortable solidity and stripped-down performance. In 1957, the 55 cu.in. ohv Sportster was introduced. It naturally didn't lose the hydraulic front fork of the Glides, but it gained a higher compression ratio after the first year and its unit construction engine, 3.0 × 3.81 in. bore and stroke, provided 40 bhp and some excellent quarter-mile times. Essentially, H-D had kept all that had been good about the KH – such as unit construction and four single-lobe cams – and converted to ohv. The larger bore meant more power and the shorter stroke meant more rpms, which meant more of the same. The engine was called the XL – X following the U and V flatheads sequence. The XLH – H for extra power with a compression ratio of 9:1 – was introduced in 1958, followed by the XLCH, which meant effectively a stripped Sportster as originally produced by the California dealers and subsequently provided by the company. The XLCH had a peanut tank to replace the extra-large heavy gauge 4.4-gallon version on the XLH, alloy wheel rims instead of steel, magneto ignition instead of coil, and lower gearing. It is impossible to be

PREVIOUS PAGES: The Sportster got a good start in life because of the lessons learned on the KH, and it kept on getting better. This chromed beauty is on Daytona Beach.

OPPOSITE AND BELOW: The Sportster, just like the big V-twins has always lent itself to individual adornment. The 1968 model opposite is mostly stock, but the owner is clearly a chrome freak.

LEFT: The XLH Sportster was introduced in 1958 with a higher compression ratio.

definitive because the H-D option list was so long. But there is no doubt that it is the XLCH which opens up a whole new chapter in Harley-Davidson history.

At 883cc, the Sportster (what a perfect name, in the same league as Vincent Black Shadow and Norton Commando) came in under the insurance limit for 900cc machines. The initial 7.5:1 compression ratio had been over-cautious for an ohv layout and the change to 9:1 caused no problems. The light alloy pistons were domes and the chambers hemispherical. The rocker arms were located in new rocker boxes and the pushrods were also light alloy. It would be difficult to imagine a more desirable home-grown machine with which to tempt the young bloods into penury. The original off-road pretensions of the machine, with knobbly tires and automotive-type shocks under the seat, became more or less irrelevant as the owners used the new power for asphalt performance, some for drag racing. It wasn't only the Sportsters that were used for this new form of competition, of course. Mike Tucker took a standard FLH, stripped it and tuned it to produce some awesome acceleration; and others bored out the big twins to the limit, or even, in Bob George's case, put in an extra engine. It isn't difficult to see the link between these stripped down dragsters and the burgeoning chopper community.

The Triumphs and Nortons still had the edge with their refined suspensions, but on

HARLEY

PREVIOUS PAGES: **The fifties style is essential to H-D products today; a panhead California custom bobber with ape hangers and hand gearchange.**

the long, empty roads of the south-west, nothing could touch the Sportster for torque and top speed. To look ahead a little into the next chapter, in 1965 the six-volt system would be replaced with 12 volts on the XLH and the XLCH magneto ignition was dropped in favor of battery ignition in 1969.

Meanwhile, the Hydra-Glide had become the Duo-Glide in 1958, the solid rear end disappearing to be replaced by swinging arm suspension, to return, or at least appear to return, three decades on. Two years before, the doughty panhead got high-lift cams for a significant power increase. Some fine tank graphics in silver, gold and black marked the FLs and FLHs at the end of the decade,

along with even bigger fins for better cooling.

It would take the British the whole of the next decade to catch up with the Sportster in terms of top speed, by which time, of course, it was no longer a two-horse race. The Kawasaki two-stroke threes and Honda fours were practically a generation ahead measured by that yardstick. The Honda 50 was announced at the end of 1959, a moped-like machine which didn't seem to have much to do with the American market. Surprisingly, America (and the rest of the world) took to it. Have a guess how many Honda 50s have been sold to date. I bet you've underestimated.

ABOVE: 1959 FLH Duo-Glide: suspension at both ends. Such wanton luxury.

DUO-GLIDE
HARLEY-DAVIDSON

CHAPTER SIX

VIVA ITALIA?

The 1960s

The lightweight and middleweight problem for Harley-Davidson was not going to go away: in fact, it was about to get a lot worse as the Japanese began to prime the market with some superb advertising for the smaller machines. In 1960, Harley-Davidson produced their first and last scooter, the Topper – "Tops under the Christmas tree this year because it's tops in appearance and tops in performance" – a 10 cu.in. two stroker with automatic transmission and a more than acceptably styled fiberglass body. But it had arrived on a dying scooter market and lasted only to 1964. The Topper wasn't the answer of course, and was never intended to be. Perhaps the pressing needs of an Italian company at that time would provide a convenient solution, beneficial to both parties.

Aeronautica Macchi SpA – Aermacchi – were the premier Italian producers of fighter aircraft during the war. Afterwards, they had been obliged to diversify into shipbuilding and motorcycles. After a faltering beginning, their race-developed Chimera 250 and then the 175cc Ala Rossa and 250 Ala Verde were in production. By the end of the 1950s, the aviation side of the business had been re-established and a new deal was in place with Lockheed. This agreement obliged the Italian company to separate its aviation and motorcycle arms.

Enter Harley-Davidson, hungry for products to replace their own, now outdated lightweight, the Hummer. A new stockholding company was created, capital provided 50-50 by H-D and Aermacchi, and the Ala Verde began to be built for sale in the US as the Sprint. The single cylinder four-stroke Sprint (and in 1962 the competition/scrambler Sprint H) sold well, despite the competition from Honda, and despite the fact that practically all of the machine except the engine was put together from bits and pieces from many not very reliable Italian suppliers. Bore was 2.598 in., stroke 2.835 in., actual displacement 246.2 cc. The 8.5:1 compression ratio of the Sprint was upped to 9.2:1 on the Sprint H. The bobbed fenders and high exhausts of the H, which outsold the standard model, looked the part, and stood comparison with the Japanese machines in looks, if not in electrics. By 1965, and now officially known as the Scrambler, a 27mm Dell'Orto carburetor and high compression ratio were providing 35 bhp. With a bigger bore for 1966, the machine was still around in 1969 as the SS 350 cc street model, still hanging in there as the SX with a new engine in 1972. That kind of longevity implies nothing but success for the Italian connection right from the word go – and without mentioning the M-50/ M-65/Shortster family, the 1970 off-road Baja, or the Rapido – all from the same source.

However, while the sales figures show that the Italian-made machines did indeed penetrate the lightweight and middleweight markets, the marriage of the old and

PREVIOUS PAGES: The reliability and solidity of the Duo-Glide lent itself to police work, as this 1960 panhead testifies.

RIGHT: Harley-Davidson's first, and last, venture into the scooter field suffered from a decline in the market as a whole, a market that was, in any case, dominated by the Italians.

27U
CLN

27

LEFT: The Sprint was Harley-Davidson's first co-venture wlth Aermacchi. The re-titled Ala Verde did well despite fierce opposition from Honda and an acutely unreliable source of Italian parts.

Harley-Davidson

SPRINT C 1962

The first Aermacchi/Harley-Davidson machine appeared in 1961. In 1969 the engine displacement rose to 350 cc, the SS 350 and SX 350 surviving until the mid-seventies.

Designations	C, H, SS, SX
Engine	ohv single 4-stroke
Bore & stroke	2.60 × 2.84 in.
Displacement	250 cc
Suspension	telescopic forks, swing-arm rear
BHP	18
Top speed	75 mph

ABOVE: Fred Warr (partnered by B.J.B. Morle) finished sixth on this 883cc XLCH Sportster in the 1000 km race for production machines at Silverstone, England, 20 May 1961.

Harley-Davidson

"TOPPER" SCOOTER 1960

Harley-Davidson's first, and only, venture into the scooter market was dropped in 1964.

Designations	60-A, 60-AU
Engine	single 2-stroke (scooter)
Bore & stroke	2.375 × 2.281 in.
Displacement	10 cu.in.
BHP	5 or 9 (depending on model)

ABOVE: **While a brave effort to break into the scooter market, the Topper lacked the lines and styling of its European counterparts.**

ABOVE: **Powered by a horizontal four-stroke, single cylinder engine, the Sprint was a useful addition to the Harley-Davidson stable, spreading the range into the bottom end of the market.**

new worlds was not an unqualified success. Sales of the Sprint were adequate, but not spectacular, partly because the dealers naturally preferred selling the larger and more profitable twins, partly because of occasionally dubious build quality, and mostly because the price could not be maintained against the Japanese competition. Entry-level machines are obviously more price-sensitive than big V-twins. The M50 moped, introduced in 1964, had three speeds, while similar machines from Japan had five. The success H-D enjoyed with Aermacchi-inspired machines in competition, entering Grand Prix racing in 1960, was eclipsed by the arrival of the Japanese ohc two-stroke racers towards the end of the decade. That said, Harley-Davidson was generally pleased with the transatlantic tie-up, and it continued under AMF until 1978; in 1974 a record 45,000 machines were built at the Varese factory.

Aermacchi isn't the whole lightweight/middleweight story for H-D in the 1960s. The US-constructed 175cc Cat was produced in 1962 for those riders not quite ready for the 250/350cc Sprint. The Cat/Pace/Ranger/Scat range used the same base to hit different, distinct markets. The Pacer was a street machine with a low-level exhaust system. The Ranger was an off-road dirt bike with 18-in. wheels and no lights, available only in 1962. The Scat was specifically designed as an on/off road "convertible", a forerunner of the 1970s trail bikes. The "solid" rear ends were softened by a pair of springs under the engine unit. In 1966, H-D tried to update the look of the range with the Bobcat, with fiberglass tanks and front guard. With Aermacchi/Harley-Davidson models established, so the Bobcat became less viable and was a swansong for the Milwaukee minnows.

Harley-Davidson

175CC "BOBCAT" 1966

Part of a range that included the "Ranger", "Pacer" and "Scat", these 175cc machines were available between 1962 and 1966.

Designations	n/a
Engine	single 2-stroke
Bore & stroke	2.375 × 2.406 in.
Displacement	175 cc
Suspension	Hydraulic front forks, swing-arm rear
BHP	30
Top speed	60 mph

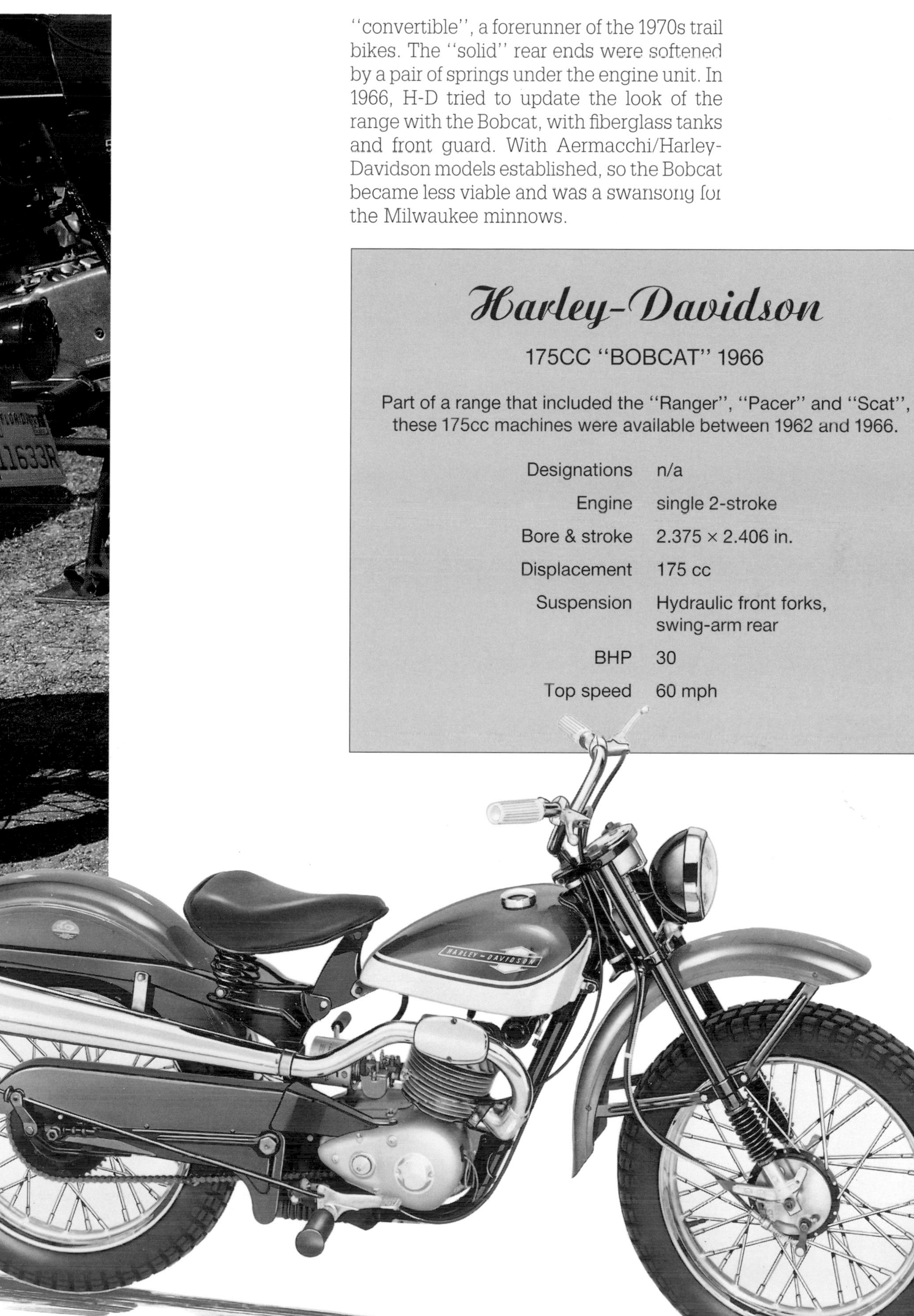

ABOVE: In the early sixties Harley-Davidson produced many accessories and novelties, allowing riders to customize their mounts according to taste and conditions.

RIGHT: To reflect the company's diversification into other fields the familiar bar and shield was dropped as the corporate logo. In its place came the stylized 'Harley-Davidson' and elongated triangles.

OPPOSITE: Motorcycles like the Duo-Glide helped the American company hold up against British rivals like Triumph during the 1960s.

Back to the big boys. For a start, William G. Davidson, son of William H., joined the company in 1962 as Director of Styling. Willie G. would have a profound effect on all of the company's products to the present day. One of his first moves was to introduce a new logo to reflect the diversifications of the company into the golf cart business, replacing the bar and shield that had been around since the 1900s, but which would survive in various forms on the motorcycles and accessories and come storming back as part of the "new nostalgia."

In 1963 the Duo-Glide gained a fish-tail muffler and better brakes. You could get fiberglass saddlebags, which were not to everyone's taste, but doubtless available because H-D had bought into the new technology by acquiring a controlling stake in the Tomahawk Boat Company, who knew all about molded plastics. The golf carts and utility trucklets produced at the Tomahawk plant were a serious money spinner. The most important change – again, deemed worthy of a name change, just like Hydra-Glide in 1949 – was that the big twin got electric starting and became the Electra-Glide in 1965. (The hyphen was

TRIUMPH

74FLH 1966

1966 was the first year for the shovelhead engine, with more horses than the panhead, useful as touring accessories became more popular.

Designations	FL, FLH
Engine	ohv V-twin
Bore & stroke	3.43 × 3.96 in.
Displacement	74 cu. in.
Suspension	telescopic forks
BHP	FL 53, FLH 60
Top speed	90 mph

dropped later.) Twelve-volt electrics and a push-button start just about put the tin hat on it. What more could you want? A sealed and enclosed primary chain? Fair enough, we've been a little slow on that one as well as with the electric start, in comparison with some manufacturers. But now, it's all there. The FLH 74 cu.in. with highway package was the biggest machine around. And this in itself caused a problem.

That old panhead was having to work harder than ever so it was time for a change. In 1966 the third new top end made its entrance: the shovelhead, with rocker boxes, not covers, and rocker arms pivoting on shafts which led to castings on the heads, looked like the back of a coal shovel. Hmmm. It's a great name for a big motorcycle powerplant, nevertheless. The extra weight of the larger battery and the starter motor initially disguised the extra power of the new engine. As (almost) always with H-D, it must be pointed out that this was not a completely new piece of kit. There was plenty of the panhead still in there.

The Sportster's new carb and cams in the same year offered a significant increase in power, and in 1967 the XLH also gained an electric starter. "Push the button . . . ZAP . . . and away you go. It's electrifying . . . It's unbelievable . . . It's new SPORTSTER H instant starting . . . Stand back . . . Take a look! . . . New Headlight Nacelle is really a beauty." A further expansion of the facil-

RIGHT: The last of the panheads, the 1965 Electra-Glide was the first of the series to boast electric ignition.

HARLEY-DAVIDSON

RIGHT: A vividly repainted 1968 Sportster, the model would retain its popularity through numerous incarnations to the present day.

MOTOR
HARLEY-DAVIDSON
CYCLES

ities at Tomahawk provided a very cool, very 1960s fiberglass sidecar to accompany the Electra Glide. And for the 1968 Glide: "In this one motorcycle, you'll get the precise engineering of a formula racer and the handcrafted luxury of a custom cruiser." (Actually, there was no change for the '68 model year.)

690 lb of 1964 Duo-Glide panhead gets you an estimated 97 mph. What you are buying in both cases is presence, not speed. The Sportster, on the other hand, which promised and delivered top end performance, was being caught by the new vertical twin 650 and 750cc machines from Triumph, Norton and BSA. Custom H-D parts were being offered by independent suppliers to keep up with the fragile but fast British machines on a growing scale, a development which, not surprisingly, evoked thunderous disapproval from Milwaukee.

It is difficult to know just how much money was used up in designing, tooling up for, and marketing the shovelhead generation, but the cost, together with some heavy outlay on the racing department, must have depleted cash reserves. For the first time, the company "went public" to raise capital in 1965; but the voting shares were still firmly in the hands of the Harley and Davidson descendants.

Despite the issue of shares in the middle of the decade, the company was still being squeezed financially as it drew to a close. Harry Sucher in *The Milwaukee Marvel*, the most complete history of Harley-Davidson that will ever be written, quotes the alarming figure of $43,000,000 gross sales and net profit after taxes of just $1,176,000. In the black, but only just. This isn't a history of the Harley-Davidson company on the stock exchange, it's about the product; but those figures are highly relevant to what happens to that product in the following decade.

BELOW AND OPPOSITE: **The 1981 FLH classic retains the retro look, but with eighties power in the 80 cu. in. engine. The side car is an added, and for many, welcome dimension, easily dealt with by the big V-twin.**

HARLEY

CHAPTER SEVEN

COMPETITION

Racing improves the breed

The history of Harley-Davidson machines in board, flat track, TT, hill-climb, road, GP and drag racing is of course far too long and just too downright interesting to be done justice in such a short space. It deserves its own book, and has several of them, notably Alan Girdler's *Harley Racers* (Motorbooks International) and for a wider view of the American racing scene, *Classic American Racing Motorcycles* by Mick Walker (Osprey). Daytona was always a key venue for Harley-Davidson, and a uniquely American institution.

The H-D company's attitude to racing has not always been one of total commitment, for some very sound reasons. As mentioned earlier, Harley-Davidson kept competition at arm's length at its inception in the 1900s. Walter Davidson's win in the 1908 Long Island Endurance Run – against 22 other motorcycle makes – was great publicity, but racing soon left the standard production machines behind, and required special equipment. To simplify a little, Walter, Bill et al couldn't see the point of the expense of running works machines and professional riders, particularly as amateurs who did well could be used in advertising without expense and without putting the company's reputation on the line. There are parallels in all kinds of motor racing, notably with "amateur" team entries at Le Mans which actually received backing from the parent company, which was never official, just in case they blew up along the Mulsanne Straight.

In 1914, however, all this changed. If H-D were going to enter the racing arena, they would do it wholeheartedly, and the works team – the Wrecking Crew – appeared for the first time in the 1914 Dodge City 300-mile race. No laurels, but from then on, with eight-valve twins and four-valve singles which were far superior in performance to the standard road machines, the Harley-Davidson works team began to dominate. Multiple entries, through which Harley-Davidson could increase their chances of victory, became a feature. Banked board racing was frighteningly fast, and the machines, without brakes, were lapping at over a ton at the beginning of the 1920s. The ohv single, the Peashooter, wasn't available to the public, nor the multiple-valve twins. Racing was a professional closed shop dominated by Works teams, and had alienated itself from the everyday rider. In 1934, the American Motorcycling Association, (established in 1923) introduced Group C racing. This was for standard production machines, of which at least 25 had to have been offered for sale to the public. Harley-Davidson and Indian controlled the AMA by this time, and it comes as no surprise that the Classic C rules specified the use of 45 cu.in. side-valves and 30.5 cu.in. singles, because that's what they both were making. The WL 45 cu.in. H-D side-valve had been introduced in 1929. Class C was a logical extension of the thinking behind the

RIGHT: AMA road racer Nancy Delgado, 883, 1992. There have been several women racers in recent H-D history more than competent to take on the boys at "their" game.

PREVIOUS PAGES: The inimitable Joe Petrali hillclimbing in 1934. Joe had put Indian in its place in the late 1920s in the then new 21 cu. in. class, riding the ohv Peashooter, in fact shaming them out of that form of competition altogether for a time.

SHOEI
55
SPECTRO
SYED
LEATHERS
sbs
H-D
121
PowerBar
DUNLOP

83

LEFT: Hillclimbing was evidently a family sport in the 1920s.

RIGHT: On April 28, the British Douglas H. Davidson (no relation, extraordinarily enough) attained a speed in excess of 100 mph for the first time in England, at Brooklands. The factory special, based on a board track machine, lost the speed record to Herbert Le Vack the very next day on an eight-valve Indian factory racer.

BELOW: Claude Temple was Douglas Davidson's partner in the record attempt.

ABOVE: Ice racing is insane enough in a Lancia Delta or BMW 318, but it was popular in 1930s Sweden on two wheels. The phlegmatic Erik Westerberg clocked 104 mph and won at Edsviken Bay near Stockholm, precise date unknown.

RIGHT: Freddie Dixon was a British enthusiast for H-D whose career would prove to be long and illustrious, enhanced by outings on the American V-twins.

350cc "Pea Shooter" racing that had been introduced in 1925. The larger twins could be entered for TT with its twists and jumps. Alongside Class C, open capacity Class A full professional - i.e. Works team – racing continued, and Class B semi-professional events. Throughout the 1910s and 1920s Harley-Davidson competed successfully in England, which helped exports considerably.

The star of the tracks and hill climbs of the late 1920s and 1930s was undoubtedly Joe Petrali. Apart from a brief flirtation with Excelsior, Joe, who had begun racing on Indian singles, was the jewel in the H-D racing crown for more than a decade. In 1935 he won all 13 AMA National Championship 350cc dirt track races. In 1937 he took one of the new 61 ohv twins to Daytona with streamlining and set a new record of 136.183 mph. The 61EL Knucklehead owed much to his own experiments with carburation. For good measure, he took a 45 cu.in. up and down the sand for a new record of 102.04 mph. He was hillclimb National Champion for five seasons straight, 1932-1936. One of his greatest achievements was probably surviving his racing career; while the efforts to reduce speed, particularly on the board tracks, had helped to lessen the mortality rate, racing was still a perilous game. Leslie "Red" Parkhurst, a stalwart of the prewar and postwar Works team took a spill in 1915 at Rockford, Illinois which was supposed to have, quite literally, dislodged his brain! It didn't warn him off though, and he returned to campaign a 61 cu.in. machine, establishing new speed records at Daytona in 1920. Most of Joe Petrali's success was garnered without factory backing; in the 1930s, hardly surprisingly, both Indian and H-D had pressing business to attend to, and factory support had more or less vanished by the late 1930s. Though in 1937 H-D produced the WLDR 45 with aluminum heads, (and the same designation again in 1940) but for a hotter machine designed for racing. In 1941, the company produced the

Harley-Davidson

21A "PEASHOOTER" 1926

The "Peashooter" achieved fame when Joe Petrali won every AMA dirt track race on one (Peashooter=ohv) during the 1935 season. Overseas markets loved it.

Designations	A, AA, B, BA
Engine	side-valve or ohv single
Bore & stroke	2⅞ × 3¼ in.
Displacement	21 cu.in.
Suspension	springer front forks
BHP	10
Top speed	approx. 50 mph (side-valve) 60 mph (ohv)

ABOVE: Joe Petrali took the mile record in March 1936 at Daytona Beach at 136.18 mph; but not with the streamlining pictured here. This is a publicity shot – the fairings made the machine unstable, and Joe had them removed.

WR, a true racer. There was a racing department under Harvey (Hank) Syvertson, who had prepared the machinery for Joe Petrali's record attempts, but it didn't run a team, it prepared machinery and sold it, or sometimes loaned it, to deserving causes. The 45 cu.in. Indian Scout had been running away from the W series H-D machinery, and the company didn't like it. By this time, board racing had faded to be replaced by flat, or dirt, track. Two versions of the racing model were produced, the WR for flat track, and the WRTT. Still, side-valves like the WL production machine but with magneto ignition, improved valve configuration and cams, larger ports, with a strengthened, lighter framc were provided for the WR.

How did they do? Well, the history of Daytona Beach as the classic road race, (albeit half on sand) begins in 1937, and a glance at the results tells the story. A battle with Indian, the British spoiling the party, then disaster in 1952, but a win out of nowhere in 1953. It wasn't really out of nowhere of course. For some time the WR 45s hadn't been quick enough to catch the Nortons and Triumphs. The Featherbed Manx Norton, with its double loop main members,

Harley-Davidson

"HILLCLIMBER" 1929

Based on the 74, the "Hillclimber's" low gearing allowed the motorcycle to climb very steep gradients in competition.

Designations	n/a
Engine	double ohv V-twin
Bore & stroke	$3^7/_{16} \times 4$ in.
Displacement	74 cu. in.
Suspension	leading link forks
BHP	unknown
Top speed	variable

BELOW: Edward James of Elmira in a spot of hillclimbing trouble Onandaga Hill.Situations like this made hillclimbing popular with spectators.

curling round from the top of the steering head, down and around, back to the base of the steering head, (chrome-molybdenum, high-tensile Reynolds 531) was a brilliantly simple base for racing success. The "Garden Gate" frame and the double ohc engine was too reliable and too fast. Similarly, the Indian Scout 45 cu.in. 648 racers had been ahead of the game.

The turning point had come in 1952 with the Harley-Davidson Model K, a machine which represented the most extensive redesign ever carried out by the company on the trusty V-twin. Although it was still a 750cc side-valve, as in the W series, a lot of it was new, notably unit construction of engine, gearbox and clutch assemblies. There was a foot change, a double loop cradle frame, swinging arm rear suspension and telescopic front forks. In addition to the basic roadster line, the new K generation was also offered as the KRTT road racer/TT model and the KR rigid-framed flat tracker.

Technically, the racing KRTT/KR engines differed from their roadster brothers in detail rather than basics. However, the competition models did not become available until August 1952, the result being that K-series bikes didn't really feature in serious competition until the following year.

The high point of the 1953 Harley-Davidson racing effort came at the Daytona 200, with Paul Goldsmith's victory, at a new race record average of 94.45 mph – made all the sweeter following several years of British victories. A special off-road competition model intended for scrambling and desert racing, the KRM, was built, but proved uncompetitive, being too heavy to succeed against the more nimble British 500 cc singles and 650 cc vertical twins.

The 1954 Daytona 200-miler witnessed a

ABOVE: The British are coming . . . The first (startling) Norton victory at Daytona on the beach/road course was in 1941. They took the first three places in 1949, and the 500cc Manx Nortons would figure in the top places until 1953, when the cudgel was taken up by BSA.

61 KR
OWNER BUILDER JOHN OLSEN
21
8
5

Harley-Davidson

KR750 1960

This was *the* dirt-track racing Harley between 1952 and 1968 when the XR re-established the make's dominance in racing.

Designations	n/a
Engine	ohv V-twin
Bore & stroke	2.74 × 3.81 in.
Displacement	750 cc
Suspension	telescopic front forks
BHP	50
Top speed	125 mph

LEFT: 1961 KR; a competition jack-of-all-trades.

reversal in fortunes for the Milwaukee V-twins, with BSA scooping the first five places, a feat not repeated until the rise of Yamaha some two decades later. However, British bike fans were to be disappointed as the rest of the AMA's racing season was dominated by Joe Leonard riding a Harley KR. Leonard won eight out of a total of 18 events in the 1954 championship calender, including the Laconia '100'. Joe Leonard was also the first man to become AMA National Champion on his cumulative season record rather than from a single race, as had been the practice in previous years.

Tom Sifton, formerly a San José motorcycle dealer, was the man who tuned Leonard's engine. Sifton's engineering skill gave Leonard an engine which offered around 50 bhp at the rear wheel – outstanding for a 750 side-valver in the early 1950s. His main efforts to improve power output had gone into porting the cylinders, improving cam profiles and fitting dual coil valve springs, the latter from the noted Triumph expert, Tom Witham. Other improvements concerned sodium-filled valves, chrome-plated stainless piston rings and the use of 5/16-in. big-end rollers in place of the original smaller diameter 3/16-in. components. The latter modification was subsequently adopted by the factory themselves.

At the end of the 1954 season Tom Sifton was persuaded to part with his super special KR Leonard motor, in fact he sold the complete machine to his friend and Harley-Davidson dealer, Leonard Andres. Andres' son Brad was then about to start his first

OPPOSITE, BELOW: The racing KRs would be transformed when the side-valve configuration (shown here) gave way to ohv.

LEFT: Vintage 1967 KRT "Lowboy" road racer in action, owned by Walt Schaefer.

Harley-Davidson

XR750 1970

A mainstay of the Harley-Davidson racing stable, the XR750 dominated the flat-tracks.

Designations	n/a
Engine	ohv V-twin
Bore & stroke	3.125 × 2.98 in.
Displacement	750 cc
Suspension	telescopic front forks
BHP	60
Top speed	145 mph

ABOVE: Dirt tracker Mert Lawwill of Tiburon, CA, H-D factory team racer of the 1960s, and one of the many great competitors who established a long-standing allegiance to Milwaukee.

season in the AMA expert ratings. The Sifton-tuned ex-Leonard machine proved its worth by assisting the 19-year-old Andres junior to win the 1955 Daytona 200-miler at a record average speed of 94.57 mph. Brad Andres went on to win several other events on the AMA championship trail, including the Laconia '100', Dodge City '75' and the famous Langhorne '100'. He emerged at the season's close as the AMA No.1 plate holder the only 'rookie' ever to have done so, Everett Brasher was second, with Joe Leonard third. All three were Harley-Davidson mounted; in fact only two events in the 17-round series went to non-Harley-Davidson riders that year.

This level of success brought about a change in the rule book in November 1955; at their annual conference AMA officials voted to allow the maximum allowable compression ratio for the following season to be raised from 8:1 to 9:1, a decision which only helped Harley's British rivals. It should be noted that the KRs were then running a compression ratio in the region of 6.5:1.

The compression ratio allowance proved of little help to the opposition as the 1956 season was to reveal – H-D machinery taking all seven title rounds. Although Joe Leonard won only two, the Mile at San Mateo, California and the TT at Peoria, Illinois, he still amassed enough points to reclaim the AMA No.1 from Brad Andres who finished second in the championship race. In 1957, Leonard not only won the championship, but half of the eight races, including his first Daytona 200 victory. For a change his nearest challenger was not another Harley man, but Al Gunter. Gunter, who was later to win fame on four wheels, rode a 499 cc Gold Star; another Beeza rider, Dick Klamfoth was third. Most noteworthy was the emergence of Carroll Resweber who finished fourth, his points tally including two national victories: the half-miles at Columbus, Ohio and St. Paul, Minnesota. The year 1957 also saw veteran Harley-Davidson race chief Hank Syvertson retire, to be replaced by Dick (OB) O'Brien.

The following year, 1958, Carroll Resweber was champion, a position he was to hold for a record-breaking four seasons in a row, all on Harley-Davidson machinery. However, that first year's title was anything but easy, Resweber scoring 36 points to Leonard's 35, and the former champion was sidelined for half the season through injury. This was to be a familiar pattern over the next four years, Resweber taking the championship, Leonard running him close. As for the foreign invaders, BSA was the main challenge to Harley-Davidson supremacy, with its Gold Star single and ohv twins scoring several individual national victories.

During Resweber's reign (1958-1961) Harley's other leading riders (besides Joe Leonard) were Brad Andres, Everett Brasher, Duane Buchanan, Troy Lee, Bart Markel and Roger Reiman. The last two individuals were both destined to become future AMA champions.

April 1960 brought news of the link-up between the Italian Aermacchi company and the Milwaukee factory. This gave Harley-Davidson the chance to market (and race) Aermacchi machinery in the USA.

The 1962 season got underway with Don Burnett winning the coveted Daytons 200-miler on a 500 Triumph twin, ending a string of seven consecutive Harley victories in this famous event. The year's AMA champion was 27-year-old Bart Markel from Flint, Michigan. Bart took over from Carroll Resweber when the four-time champ was involved in an horrific accident at the Lincoln, Illinois five-mile championship race in September. At that time Resweber led Markel 44 points to 40 and it had appeared that Resweber was heading for his fifth consecutive No.1 plate. But this was not to be. Jack Goulsen, Dick Klamfoth and Resweber all went down heavily during a practice lap. Goulson was killed instantly, Resweber in-

BELOW: Walter Villa at the 1976 West German 250cc Grand Prix at Hockenheim. He won, helped, no doubt, by the Campagnolo enclosed disc at the front and the square section swinging arm.

Harley-Davidson

CRTT ROAD RACER 1963

Racing versions of the Aermacchi 250 cc single Sprint.

Designations	CR, CRTT, CRS
Engine	ohv single
Bore & stroke	2.59 × 2.83 in.
Displacement	15 cu. in.
Suspension	telescopic forks
BHP	28
Top speed	115 mph

ABOVE: Jay Springsteen aboard a 250cc Aermacchi. Springsteen would come into his own in dirt track on XRs in the late 1970s.

jured a leg so badly that he was destined never to race again and Klamfoth was so sickened after the experience that he hung up his leathers there and then. Markel went on to take the title with 58 points, Resweber's tally staying on 44; then came Dick Mann riding a combination of BSA (Gold Star) and Matchless (G50) machinery.

Dick Mann was champion in 1963 – but only after a lot of bitter controversy concerning his Matchless G50. Mann took the title by a single point from H-D's teamsters George Roeder and Ralph White.

The rising popularity of small capacity bikes led to a 250 cc AMA National Championship. The 1963 event was staged at the Peoria, Illinois TT circuit. Bart Markel won, riding a Harley (read Aermacchi) ohv Sprint. *Cycle World* tested both the Sprint and the latest KR (actually the Jerry Branch-tuned machines raced by Dick Hammer). Both sported dolphin fairings, which the AMA had allowed from the beginning of that year in road racing events. The Sprint achieved 116 mph, the KR 142 mph. Prices for the standard over-the-counter racers were $900 and $1,295 respectively, and power output figures were quoted for the Sprint at 28.5 bhp 9500 rpm; KR 48 bhp 6800 rpm.

Some of the Sprint competition history is described in Chapter 6, particularly the amazing achievement in the mid-1970s of Walter Villa, Harley-Davidson's multiple World Champion. But the effort began in 1960 with Grand Prix entries of the ohv flat single "Ala Verde" – remember, for production machines, Ala Verde = 250 Sprint in the US, ridden by Alberto Pagani. Fifth at Spa Francorchamps in Belgium that year, behind three MV Agustas and Mike Hailwood (fourth) on a Ducati twin. Not impressed? Everyone was at the time: the Ardennes course is notoriously fast and the new kid on the block had really surprised the established works teams. Bore and stroke were changed for 1962 and power upped to 28 bhp at 9500 rpm, plus a much-needed five-speed gearbox. You could buy one and race it yourself in 1961 if you had the money – and could find a machine. The company underestimated demand, always a gratifying and agonizing experience. Factory-supported riders competed in Europe only in GP for 1964, and won incredible fourth places in the German and Italian GPs. The engine grew to 380 or 402 cc for European racing before the end of the decade, but the introduction of the Yamaha and TR2 twins assured the single cylinder Aermacchi machine of an honorable GP death in 1969. Five years later, the 250 water-cooled twin was ready for Walter Villa to take GP racing by storm.

The Aermacchi competition machines were not only seen in Europe; some campaigned the RR 250 (the production version of the factory racers) in AMA events in the 1970s, and a dirt tracker was developed from the SX 250 trail bike, the MX 250. The Varese racing effort would come to an end before the MX 250 could prove itself, as the transatlantic ties were severed.

Meanwhile, in 1964 Harley-Davidson returned to the top of the AMA's championship pile, the rider this time being Roger Reiman; his two victories in the 17-round series came at Daytona and the Short Track meeting at Hinsdale, Illinois. Reiman gained his title, as Mann had done the previous year, on consistency rather that outright race wins. Roger Reiman scored his second consecutive Daytona 200 victory in March 1965, but in the season-long AMA championship series it was Bart Markel who upheld Harley's honor against a flood of British bikes from BSA, Triumph and Matchless; while Dick Mann became the first rider of a Japanese machine to win an AMA National when he took his Yamaha TD1 twin to victory in the 250 cc race at Nelson Ledges, Ohio. It was also the first time a two-stroke had won an AMA National.

Markel was again No.1 in 1966, carried to success aboard the latest version of the long-running KR side-valver. But generally the American marque had a tough year with Triumph machinery taking many of the honors, including victory at Daytona. One bright note was Cal Rayborn's first National win at the Carlsbad, California road race.

By the mid-1960s, racing a side-valve anywhere outside the USA you would rightly have been considered hopelessly optimistic. FIM regulations classified engines by capacity and, on that basis, it was common knowledge that the side-valve

BELOW: Mark Brelsford, 1972 AMA Grand National Champion. AMF continued to support AMA competition practically throughout their tenure.

OPPOSITE: 1977 XR-750; perfectly street legal.

was much less efficient than the overhead valve or overhead camshaft designs. But American racing of the period was ruled by the AMA and not the FIM: the side-valve (read Harley-Davidson!) was allowed 750 cc (more with permitted over-boring) while ohv engines were limited to 500 cc.

Another restriction which had long favored the home-grown Harleys against the foreign invaders was the ceiling on compression ratios, though this had been allowed to climb slowly from 7.5:1 to 9:1 over the previous two decades. The lower figure was just about as high a ratio as could be squeezed from a tuned side-valve, with its large, sprawling valve pocket at the side of the cylinder head; but it blunted the edge of a British production racer just enough to help Harley's cause. Even so, getting a side-valve 750 through the speed traps at around 145 mph was still a marvelous achievement, especially when one considers the technical problems in tuning a side-valve for speed work.

A one-off 883 cc ohv XLR Sportster engine was fitted into a special 'Low-Boy' frame and raced by the Californian Lance Weil on British short circuits during 1967. It won 1000 cc races at Lydden Hill, Brands Hatch, Oulton Park and Mallory Park, and in the process created a considerable amount of publicity on both sides of the Atlantic.

After its defeats at the hands of Triumph during 1967, Harley-Davidson made an amazing come-back to the AMA racing scene with a revitalized KR model for 1968/69. Much of 1967 had been spent on development work by Dick O'Brien and his team of engineers. At the center of this was a 'Low Boy' chassis of the type first used on Weil's machine and special accessories such as gas tank, seat and, most important of all, a wind tunnel-tested fairing: these latter components were the work of the Wixom Bros. of Long Beach, California. Although Dick O'Brien never revealed the exact power output figures for the revised 1968 works KR, they were well over 60 bhp at the rear wheel with the rpm now up to over 7000.

Known improvements included Tillotson diaphragm carburetors, revised exhaust valve timing and new cam profiles. Also because of the new twin carb arrangement the combustion chambers and compression ratio were both altered. Proof of how effective this work had been is that Harley-Davidson gained some 8 mph on lap speeds at Daytona, with Roger Reiman setting the fastest qualifying speed for the 1968 200-miler at 149.080 mph. In the race Cal Rayborn went on to lap all but second and third by the end of 40 laps; he also became the first rider to win the event at an average speed of over 100 mph.

Only eight KR 750s were built in 1969 – all team bikes. They all employed Italian Ceriani front forks and massive Fontana four leading shoe front drum brakes, with an American-made single hydraulically-operated disc at the rear.

Cal Rayborn again dominated the proceedings at Daytona and the majority of the other road races that year, but it was fellow H-D teamster, Mert Lawwill, who took the championship with 672 points thanks to his flat track skills (a vital requirement in gaining the AMA Championship title). Rayborn finished third in the rankings with 517 points.

But 1969 was also to see the end of both the KR era (the AMA were introducing a new more open 750 category for 1970) and the company, taken over by AMF. The Harley-Davidson race shop, headed by Dick O'Brien, was faced with some real headaches, brought about by the new set of AMA rules and the fact that AMF, focused on production figures, didn't see racing as a priority. Even so, O'Brien tried. The result was first displayed to the public at the Houston Show, Texas in February 1970; the XR 750, designed by Dutchman Pieter Zylstra.

The prototype was built within a four month period. This short time and the fact that, although supposedly a new design, it owed much to the old KR side-valve (cycle parts) and the standard production XL Sportster (engine). Lined up against machines such as the BSA/Triumph triples, the Honda CB 750 four and Ducati V-twin, the 'new' Harley was obviously going to find life difficult, at least on the tarmac.

The Daytona race exemplified the 1970 season: unmitigated disaster. Officially H-D blamed piston failures, but the troubles were not that simple and far more widespread. Most of these problems centered around too much heat. The "iron" XR 750 motor soon gained a salutory nickname, the "Waffle Iron", and this was to be the prime cause of the team machines' breakdowns

during the championship season with awful regularity. Of the 25 races counting towards the AMA title, Harley-Davidson only won seven defending champion Mert Lawwill eventually finished sixth, the best of the Milwaukee teamsters. This was also the company's lowest-ever finish in the national championship.

During the closed season break, O'Brien and his men carried out a mini-redesign with reworked cylinder heads, new crank fly-wheels (forged steel and with the mainshaft also forged as an integral part of the flywheel); the heads were now held in place with long through studs into the crankcases instead of separate bolts from case to barrel and from barrel to head. But any gain made to the engine was offset by a spate of gearbox breakages, certainly for the first half of the 1971 season.

In road racing events Cal Rayborn showed himself to be a true master of the

ABOVE: 1980 XR-750 flat-tracker; in that year Randy Coss became AMA Grand National Champion.

craft, at least while his bike kept going. Even though he was down on speed he rode like no one else in Stateside road racing during 1970 and 1971, but the machine just wouldn't see it through.

The old "Waffle Iron" did have one weekend of glory, when Rayborn amazed the British by winning three of the six Anglo-American Match Races over Easter 1972 on an iron XR 750 prepared by Walt Faulk. The British team included the likes of multi-world champion Phil Read, Peter Williams, John Cooper and Ray Pickrell; and it was this latter rider who provided the main challenge that weekend.

Long before the Rayborn foray across the Atlantic, Harley-Davidson had decided something must be done to salvage their tarnished racing reputation. That something was the new alloy-engined XR 750, which appeared in time for the 1972 AMA championship season. Unfortunately for Cal Rayborn and H-D, the large capacity Japanese two-strokes, not to mention the new wave European 750 four-strokes, were by this time also on the American scene in great numbers. There were now Yamaha, Suzuki and Kawasaki two-strokes in addition to the four-strokes, such as the BSA/Triumph triples.

The first the world saw (and it was only a glimpse) of the prototype alloy-engined XR was at Ontario in October 1971. Then it was tucked away inside the big Harley-Davidson race transporter. Before Ontario this engine had been tested on a one-mile dirt track, but never on any sort of road course. However, Harley's Dick O'Brien told members of the press that the team intended to stay at Ontario after the meeting so that Rayborn and Brelsford could make tests.

Besides riders such as Rayborn and Brelsford, Harley were also able to call on the services of the Italian star Renzo Pasolini, thanks to the Aermacchi connection. Pasolini proved himself a quick learner and, although Kawasaki won the important Ontario F 750 event (run in two heats due to concern over tire wear), Pasolini was Harley's best result with third overall.

Following Rayborn's superb showing in the 1972 Easter Match Races, he returned to England that September for the Race of the Year at Mallory Park. This time he had one of the latest model alloy-engined XR 750s and full factory support (something he didn't have for his original visit)). In the race he duelled with Yamaha works GP star, Jarno Saarinen, until the Harley's magneto expired.

After the lean years of 1970 and 1971, 1972 was a relief, with Mark Brelsford becoming the new AMA national champion. The Harley rider scored a total of 1483 points; the nearest challenger was Triumph-mounted Gary Scott on 1105. Other leading contenders that year included Gene Romero (Triumph), Kenny Roberts (Yamaha), Chuck Palmgren (Yamaha), Dick Mann (BSA), Jim Rice (BSA) plus the Harley trio of Mert Lawwill, Cal Rayborn and Dave Sehl.

The following year was to prove a poor season for the Milwaukee marque. Even on the dirt, the combination of Kenny Roberts and Yamaha XS 650 vertical twin proved a serious threat to H-D's former invincibility in this particular branch of the sport. Typical of the 1973 season for Harley was the Daytona 200. Brelsford qualified at 97.954 mph (Rayborn's qualfying speed was 98.503 mph) and suffered a truly horrendous accident on lap 11 of the race, in which his machine became a fireball and he sustained two broken legs, a broken hand and a badly damaged kneecap, which sidelined the 1972 AMA Grand Champion for the rest of the year.

Later in the race Rayborn's engine seized, throwing him off the bike. In the incident he landed heavily, breaking his collarbone and suffering damaged ribs. Cal came back too soon, his collarbone not fully mended, and another incident aggravated matters. History records that he went to England as captain of the US squad in the annual Anglo-American Match Race Series: what most people don't know is that he rode with his collarbone still broken and was in considerable pain.

In road racing for 1973, the faster and lighter two-stroke competition was much more competitive. Even Rayborn's undoubted skill couldn't make the difference. Rayborn was so frustrated by this state of affairs that he quit Harley-Davidson at the end of that year. Tragically, the 33-year-old Californian was killed whilst on his first outing on a 500 cc Suzuki twin, crashing at the Auckland, New Zealand circuit on 1 January, 1974. The Suzuki had been loaned

BELOW: Dirt track was the main focus for H-D and for the AMA – dominated by the aforementioned – in the late 1970s and early 1980s. Why do you suppose that was?

ABOVE: Sacramento Mile, October 1992; 92 is Rodney Ferris, 66 George Roeder, and 42 is Steve Morehead. George had taken a tuned and streamlined 250cc Aermacchi Sprint to 177 mph way back in 1965 on the Bonneville Salt Flats.

RIGHT: A 1986 XR-750 flat-tracker ridden by the multi-talented Wayne Rainey.

to Rayborn so that he could compete in an international series in New Zealand. Many informed observers consider Cal Rayborn to have been America's finest road racer of the pre-Grand Prix era and the precursor of riders such as Roberts, Spencer, Lawson, Rainey and Schwanz. Certainly Calvin Rayborn was Harley-Davidson's finest-ever road racer, and a great sportsman to boot.

Following Rayborn's departure and subsequent fatal accident, the Milwaukee factory never repeated its road successes and (except for Battle of the Twins racing) never gained another Daytona victory with the V-twin.

Harley-Davidson still produced its share of AMA champions once Kenny Roberts had departed to Europe during the late 1970s and into the 1980s, but these victories were thanks to performances on the dirt. This is where we came in. Remember that in the immediate postwar period five types of 'racing' made up the AMA Championship. One was America's own stone-age version of road racing – in which the combatants campaigned standard issue dirt track irons and even dragged their feet through the turns. The other four, which were to remain a vital facet of Stateside competition, were half-mile, mile, short track and, most exciting of all, the TT steeplechase. The latter (no relation to the Isle of Man TT) comprised both right and left turns plus a mighty jump in which riders shoot 30 or 40 feet at crowd-pleasing speed.

For short track events, engine sizes varied through the years before finally settling on a standard 250 cc maximum. Other types of dirt track racing were open to two classes, originally 45 and 80 cubic inch. But before long, rules for the national series were standardized and the maximum engine capacity was set at 750 cc. As with speedway, the machine had no brakes (rear brakes were allowed from 1970). As a result the racing was quite unique and, with speeds of over 120 mph on the longer tracks, exciting in the extreme; imagine a massive Harley V-twin drifting sideways and broadside at three figure speeds, full lock broadslides being needed to scrub off speed in lieu of braking equipment.

Up to the end of the 1960s Harley-Davidson, with their KR 750 V-twins and the Italian-built 250 cc ohv Sprints, were usually the front runners, British bikes led by Triumph and BSA never far behind.

With the advent of the 1970s the new ohv XR 750 made its debut on dirt as well as tarmac, together with a fresh set of challengers from Japan and Europe. In the big class the XR 750 soon became a much more successful bike on the dirt than it was ever to become on the tarmac; first in the hands of Mark Brelsford and Gary Scott and later Jay Springsteen, Steve Eklund, Randy Goss,

BELOW: Jay "Springer" Springsteen pictured with an 883 flat-tracker in 1993. Jay's advertising contribution to H-D cannot be measured in mere dollars.

RIGHT: Sturgis, 1992 (Rat's Hole). The H-D dragsters always steal the show.

ABOVE: In 1990 the RS 1200 Westwind was announced, designed by Erik Buell; it's a supersports machine, but it's still, strictly speaking, a road bike. Will Harley-Davidson ever compete in Grand Prix? The immediate answer is no – but a lot can happen in another 90 years.

Ricky Graham and finally Scott Parker.

Of these H-D dirt specialists, the greatest has to be Jay "Springer" Springsteen. Springer had that rare talent, as displayed by the likes of Leonard Resweber and Markel in earlier days, of a totally fearless ability to put his Harley V-twin in front of the pack and stay there, come-what-may, until the chequered flag finally goes down.

Thanks to men like these no other manufacturer comes anywhere near Harley-Davidson's record in AMA racing; they were to America what MV Agusta were to

Europe in the classic period from 1945 until the end of the 1970s.

For the eighties, the H-D action was in Battle of the Twins, as the XR 750 dirt track triumphs came to an end with the dominance of Honda (RS750) from 1984 onwards. The AMA series allowed Harley-Davidson back into the road racing scene, a series for souped-up production machinery, 1000cc limit. It was a way of shaking up the dominance of Yamaha and the two-stroke multivalve racers from Suzuki and Kawasaki. The four-stroke twins could now show their mettle, and not surprisingly it quickly became a popular series in the States and in Britain. In 1983, Jay Springsteen (who else) won the BOT at Daytona. The basis of the machine was the XR1000, described in Chapter Nine. The rider Gene Church pulled off a series of victories in the Grand Prix class BOT series in the ensuing years. The 883 class allowed the little machines their moments of glory. Ducati were the serious opposition, and had won the first BOT in 1982. The World Superbike series provided another outlet for H-D to compete on an even footing.

What's happening now? Well, BOT is still here, and perhaps one example will suffice to give a flavor of what's on offer on a small scale. H-D, obviously, are never going to mix it in GP or anything like it for as far ahead as anyone can see. In Britain, though, if you want to go racing, you can try the BEARS or clubman's 883 Sportster Series. If you reach the flag first at Knockhill or Cadwell Park, you'll pick up 20 points and £200 ($300); the races are not yet at national level. The British magazine *Motorcycle Sport* used some extraordinary words to characterise the 883 Series in its November 1993 issue: "camaraderie, friendliness, and all-round sportsmanship," words that cast these modern races back to another age.

BELOW: Nigel Gale competing on an 883 racer. Harley-Davidson have always had an ambivalent attitude toward competition – quite rightly today, in view of the realities of their product – but if you want to see the V-twins in action, it's still possible, if you know where to look.

CHAPTER EIGHT

AMERICAN MACHINE AND FOUNDRY

1969 – 1980

HARLEY DAVIDSON
Fairing
OIL PRESSURE
MPH
Harley-Davidson

Remember Harley Davidson's extraordinary export successes achieved at various stages in its history, from the 1920s onwards? By the mid-1960s sales outside the USA and Canada amounted to just three percent of total production. This state of affairs was revealed by the necessary public declaration of the financial position of the company before takeover by American Machine and Foundry.

As stated earlier, this book is not a financial analysis, but it's probably fair to say that bankruptcy was a very real threat in 1968, just as it had been in 1932. The damage this time was not worldwide depression; in fact the motorcycle market had been expanding incredibly quickly as leisure dollars had become available through the growth of the US economy. This time the problem was fairly and squarely imports, which had limited H-D's market share, and had corralled them in the big twin stockade. The British, the Germans, the Italians, and from the end of the 1950s, the Japanese, not only threatened Harley-Davidson's business but, ironically, were responsible for the expansion of the US motorcycle market. Yamaha, for example, just like H-D, had produced its own version of the German DKW RT125 in the 1950s. That was its first machine. In the early 1960s, its scooter and moped range was a failure, more costly than H-D's efforts. But by 1973 it was offering a huge number of lightweight and middleweight machines with North America as its most important target: 24, from the YB50 and V50 to the RD350 and DT360, with TD/TZ racing machines also available. Aermacchi had helped, but hadn't really had a wide enough model range. Thus it was that the giant engineering concern, AMF, gained control of Harley-Davidson on January 7, 1969.

Another myth – like the myth of H-D the lumbering technological dinosaur – that is rapidly disappearing is the good ol' boy snarl about AMF destroying Milwaukee's finest. The real truth is that not only did they, to all intents and purposes, save it, they re-established it with massive investment in plant and machinery for the *risorgimento* of the 1980s. What went wrong, maybe, was a lack of focus on the product.

In 1972 conversion of AMF's York, Pennsylvania factory for motorcycle output was begun. By 1973 production capacity had been quadrupled. The heart of the beast – the V-twin engines and transmissions – still came out of Capitol Drive. AMF bought some frighteningly expensive kit to expedite the forthcoming productivity explosion, the best example being the Cross Automated Transfer line which tooled the five-speed transmission: $4,500,000 of faith in the leisure market.

But what about the iron? It's all very well tooling up for huge numbers, but it's no good if it's huge numbers of second-rate machines. In 1970 the Sportster was restyled with a boat-tail fiberglass seat-fender

PREVIOUS PAGES: The radio and speakers of a bar-mounted FLH fairing, introduced in 1969, it was produced at the Tomahawk fiberglass plant.

RIGHT: An AMF-produced Electra Glide with shovelhead engine – and more fiberglass.

AMF

RIGHT: An interesting prototype that never made it into production: a 250 sports model with café racer styling on view at the Milan Show, 1975.

Harley-Davidson

SPORTSTER XLCH 1972

Still in production today, the series came up with the original XLCH in 1962. Tradition has it that the CH designation stood for 'Competition Hot,' but it probably doesn't.

Designations	n/a
Engine	ohv V-twin
Bore & stroke	3.18 × 3.812 in.
Displacement	61 cu. in.
Suspension	telescopic forks, swing-arm rear
BHP	60
Top speed	115 mph (claimed)

one-piece. It was not to everyone's taste, but was a gift to the aftermarket dealers and those who had stockpiled the earlier seats.

In the same year, Cal Rayborn took a fettled Sportster engine inside a CAD streamlined tube to the Bonneville Salt Flats for an assault on the world motorcycle speed record. Lying flat on his back in the orange cigar-shaped shell, (it was only two feet high) he blasted across the salt to attain a speed for the measured mile of 266.785 mph. On the return trip he obviously lost his nerve (he was steering the projectile by looking out of the side windows, so we shouldn't be too hard on him), jammed on the brakes and clocked 264.200 mph. The average speed was therefore 265.492, the fastest ever for two wheels.

The Aermacchi Baja off-roader arrived with 1000ccs and pretensions to desert racing success. The SR 100 did gain a class win in the Greenhorn Enduro, but guess which nation was improving its off-road machines year by year as the Baja remained unchanged through its five years in production? Japan's Honda, Kawasaki and now Suzuki, of course. Compression ratio was 9.5:1, bore 1.97 in., stroke 1.97 in., actual displacement 98.1cc. A machine with fewer pretensions to genuine competition success, but with more sales, the Rapido, which became the TX in 1973, the SX in 1974 and the SXT in 1975, was able to take on the Japanese at least in terms of price. The fact that the series survived in production from 1968 to 1977 speaks for itself.

Here's a good idea. It doesn't rain in Indianapolis, but it snows a lot in the north. The motorcycle, as we have seen, has not really been a utility vehicle – except for state and federal agency work – since ferrying agricultural workers down on the farm in the 1930s. So what is a motorcycle dealer to do in Seattle or even Quebec when the weather prohibits use of the motorcycle as a leisure pursuit? It was actually a Quebec company (Bombardier Ltd) that seemed to have the answer: the snowmobile. Soon, two-cylinder, two-stroke H-D engines were placed in an AMF frame (providing another use for fiberglass) and dealers were pushing them above the snowline. The effort petered out in 1975, but it did generate income, not on the scale of the golfcarts, but enough to take up a tiny proportion of the huge and growing H-D production capacity.

Back to the shovelhead. The shovelhead, introduced in 1966, had the same bore and stroke as the 74 cu.in. engines from way back in 1941, and that continued to be the case to 1969. In 1970, the D.C. generator was replaced with an A.C. unit, so the "late" engine is known as the alternator shovelhead. This change meant major surgery to the crankcases. The back-up kick start disappeared.

By 1971 the success of the chopper subculture could be ignored no longer. If that's what the people wanted, if the full "Dresser" just wasn't hitting the spot for everyone, it was foolish for the company to abandon a whole section of the market – their market; it was, after all, their products that were being messed around. The new bike wasn't called a chopper, of course; "custom" has a far gentler ring to it. Willie G took the frame and heart of the FL and married it to the front of the XL series, to create the FX 1200 Super Glide. True enough, those aluminum forks were not as downright dangerous as some you could find on the west coast; the red, white and blue colors ("Sparkling America" according to the factory) were hardly going to upset your granny, but the absence of footboards and starter motor said "this is not a Dresser, this is stripped (sort of) for action." The footpegs were directly borrowed from the choppers, longer forks obliging the rider to lean further

BELOW: Willie G., the instigator of the extraordinarily successful FX series, having fun at Daytona, 1992.

BOTTOM: Cal Rayborn and the H-D world recordbreaker at Bonneville Salt Flats.

Harley-Davidson

FX 'SUPER-GLIDE' 1972

With the frame, shovelhead engine and rear suspension from the FL, and front end from the Sportster XL, this bike saw the beginning of a whole new series of machines that would leave behind the original big Tourers in terms of production numbers.

Designations	n/a
Engine	ohv V-twin
Bore & stroke	3.43 × 3.96 in.
Displacement	74 cu. in.
Suspension	telescopic forks
BHP	65
Top speed	110 mph

back. At the same time, the Dresser market had been formalized in 1969, with the full FLH touring option including the fairing mounted on the handlebars turning with the wheel, the windshield, saddlebags in fiberglass and a third case (the "Tour-Pak") racked above the rear fender.

The Super Glide was an astute move; on the one hand, you have the relatively staid FL and FLH, on the other the Sportster, which is being challenged strongly by more powerful machines from Europe and Japan. Combine the two, lose some of the weight of the FL, avoid direct confrontation with the foreign speedsters, and you may just create your very own market niche, with a machine that will gladly accelerate away at the lights, but will also tick over in town. Which was more or less what happened. The 1970 FX (F from FLH, X from XLH) like the Sportster, had a fiberglass rear fender/ seat, which didn't look quite right and was

LEFT: A 1970 FLH, the year in which the D.C. generator on the shovelhead was replaced with an A.C. unit.

BELOW: A heavily customized 1979 Super Glide, owned by Rich Pierpont. The Super Glide Fat Bob produced at the end of the decade was designed in part to do the work for the customizers, but would certainly not be enough to satisfy this customer.

dropped for the conventional separate seat in 1972. For 1973 the suspension was firmed up and it gained disc brakes. There was no electric start, and there was quite an art to firing up, which is only fair, seeing as the FX was supposed to be more of a sports machine than the Electra Glide; but when the electric start was offered as an option (the FXE) in 1974, two out of three customers took it. 108 mph top and a 560 lb weight – halfway between the Sportster and the Glide – was just about right. In 1976 a Bicentennial Liberty Edition FXE was offered with black metallic paint. The FX would be the inspiration for the Fat Bob and the Wide Glide in a few years time. Looking back, it really comes as something of a surprise that a hybrid motorcycle like the FX should handle so well, and should hold together in looks and performance. Maybe Willie G. (a rider himself of course, in the family's finest tradition) could see it would work from the word go; maybe the test program was extensive. Either way, the Super Glide is a high point in H-D history.

At this point federal regulations concerning emissions and safety really began to bite. AMF had the money to set up state-of-the-art testing facilities to cope with the new rules. By 1978, the Ham Can air filter meant that the big V-twins would pass noise and emission laws. The Electra Glide gained a hefty 10 in. front disc brake as part

Harley-Davidson

SX 250 1975

The SX 250 was an off-road version of the SS 250 street machine.

Designations	SS/SX 250
Engine	2-stroke single cylinder
Bore & stroke	2.84 × 2.35 in.
Displacement	15 cu. in. (243 cc)
Compression ratio	10.3:1
Suspension	telescopic forks
Top speed	75 mph

ABOVE: Road-going SS 250 from 1975. The SS/SX two-stroke singles series was produced from 1974 to 1978.

of the celebrations of the 50th anniversary of the 74 cu.in. H-D motor. Harley-Davidson had always claimed that 74 was the right number for a classic tourer, and who could argue with a 50-year record? Reduced-octane fuel caused a problem which would not really be solved until the Evo engine's appearance. The Sportster got 61 cu.in. for 1972.

As for Aermacchi, they were still there, and in 1972 the SX 350, an off-road version of the Sprint appeared. In 1973 the Sprint gained a full duplex frame and 12 volts. In 1972/73, a relabelling exercise: all the light-weight model names were dropped in favor of letters and numbers. The Rapido became the TX 125: "Before you know it, you're where you want to be. Sun-drenched, tingly and feeling like new money." The SS 125 and SXT 125 of 1975 were new, and the SST 250 of the following year was the SS with discs. The 1978 SST 125 roadster did not suffer from the low-build quality of some of the Italian machines.

One of the most exciting and effective aspects of the American-Italian alliance was in competition, discussed in greater detail elsewhere, but worthy of mention in relation to how the lightweight production machinery must have been judged by the buying public. The 250cc twin cylinder road racer, the RR 250, won three consecutive 250 World Championships in the hands of the legendary Walter Villa, 1974-6. Gary Scott won the 250cc road race at Loudon on the same rig in 1974. In 1977, Walter Villa took the 350 World Championship on the RR 350. The machines had plenty of foreign blood in them, including British girling forks and Japanese Mikuni carburetors, but it was a remarkable achievement for a company that had been in the 250 market for such a short time.

Other lightweights made an appearance, the SX 175 in 1974, and the SS 175 in 1976. But two-strokes were out of favor, not least with the EPA over noise. Motorcycling didn't need a Ralph Nader to upset the apple cart; everyone was on its back anyway.

For the 1976 Bicentennial, besides the FX special, H-D pushed the boat out at Daytona Beach and set up a "Salute to American Motorcycling" in a hotel ballroom. The exhibition of old and new machinery was so successful that it become an annual event. There was also a Liberty edition of the FLH.

In 1977 Willie G. carried on with the logic behind the FX and produced the FXS Low Rider, with flat, drag-type bars, mag wheels and some suitably chic silver and red paint. The seat was scooped like a Colin Chapman racing car (such an easy and brilliant way of reducing frontal area, though in the Low Rider's case, it was for show, not to reduce drag coefficient) and the suspension shortened to bring the rider just 27 inches from the road. The Low Rider also got a sissy bar and electric start, so it wasn't really mean, it just looked that way.

The Super Glide Fat Bob appeared at the end of the decade, another attempt to preempt the customizers. The name comes from the habit of stripping everything but the big dual fuel tanks, rather than installing something off a moped: bobbed, but still fat. H-D also tried to tempt buyers with the word "Café"; a tricky word to define, but, according to Mike Clay in his book *Café Racers, Rockers, Rock 'n' Roll and the Coffee-bar Cult*, it's a bike as "a piece of pure hedonism." The black XLCR Café Racer was a little too unusual for the H-D lovers and was only offered for one model season, in 1973. It did provide something however, if not sales: a new frame, using the triangulated top rails as on the rear of the XR 750 racer. The frame was used for all the XL series from 1978.

That year was the company's 75th anniversary, and to mark the event, Willie G., Chairman John Davidson, President Vaughn Beals and a band of other executives toured the country on their various Harley-Davidsons meeting and greeting. Now that's what I call marketing.

In time for the celebrations, the anniversary model Electra Glide in black and gold traded in the 50-year-old 74 for 80 cu.in., (or more accurately, 81). 1340cc just had to come. The emissions regs demanded it for one thing, as they strangled performance. What else could be done? Actually, quite a lot; the next decade saw more radical changes to the big Twins than just about anything that happened in the 1970s.

The Wide Glide (1980), strictly speaking, should be described in the next chapter, but it's very much a part of the Super Glide/Low Rider/Fat Bob family. The 80 cu.in. Wide Glide custon, FXWG, was a Fat Bob with extended front forks, buckhorn bars, wider triple clamps, spoked 21-in. front wheel, small Sportster headlight and bobbed rear fender. You really couldn't go much further in customizing at the factory. It was a hit, just as the FX original had been. In fact, the FX machines had outsold the FL and FLHs, and the FL had actually been dropped from the model lineup.

As always – and in some ways the FX machines were part of the struggle – H-D

BELOW: A 1973 SX 350 sprint trail bike. The four-stroke from Aermacchi and the two-strokes from home were reliable machines, but sales were never huge, partly because the youth/offroad market was foreign to the dealers. In that year, for example, 2431 SX 350s were sold, as against 10,825 XLCHs.

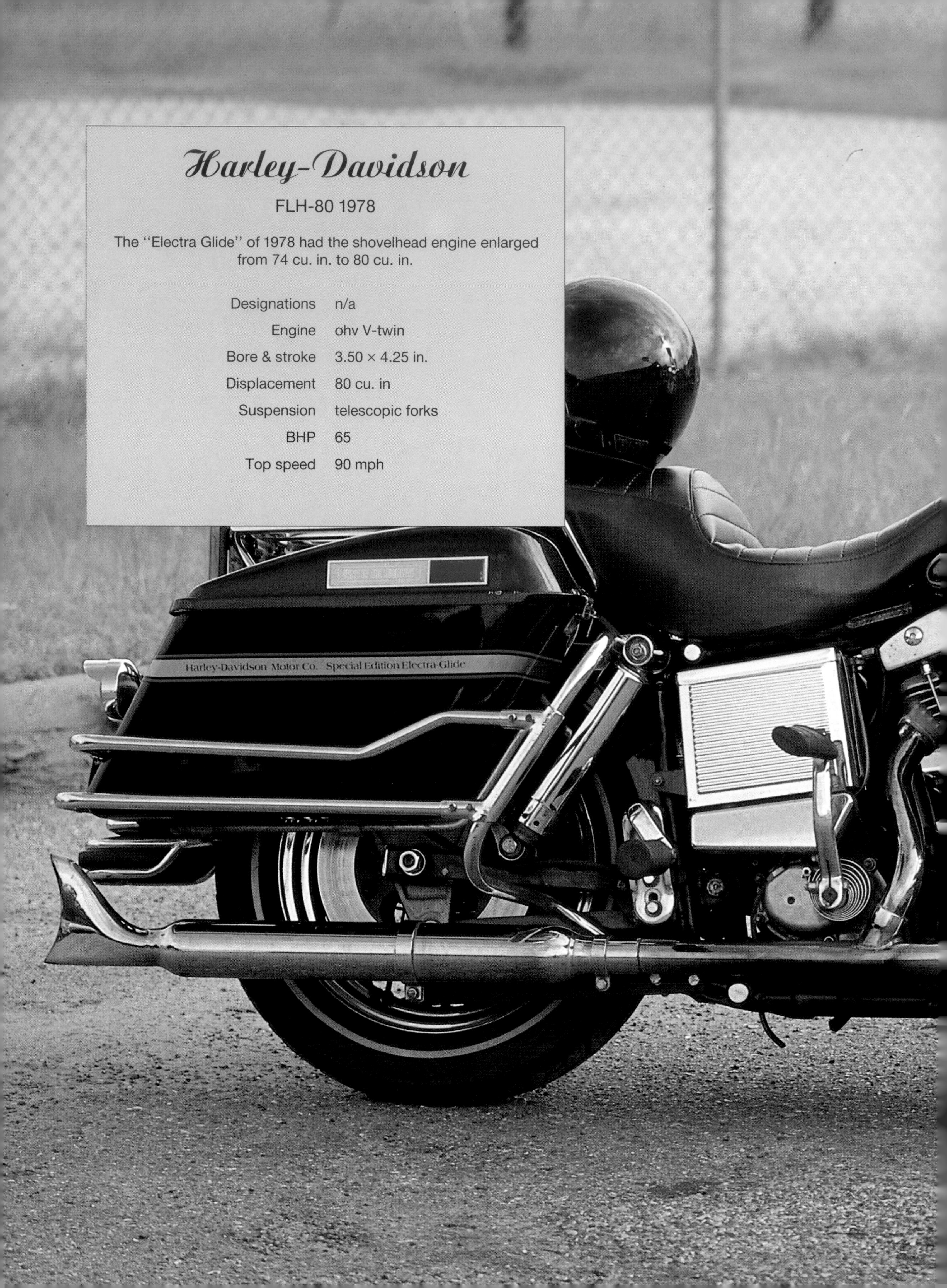

Harley-Davidson

FLH-80 1978

The "Electra Glide" of 1978 had the shovelhead engine enlarged from 74 cu. in. to 80 cu. in.

Designations	n/a
Engine	ohv V-twin
Bore & stroke	3.50 × 4.25 in.
Displacement	80 cu. in
Suspension	telescopic forks
BHP	65
Top speed	90 mph

MOTOR
HARLEY-DAVIDSON
CYCLES
Special Edition Electra-Glide
FLH

ABOVE: **1976 74 cu. in. FLH Electra Glide, but fitted with the more attractive 1978 wheels.**

PREVIOUS PAGES: **Special Edition Electra Glide.**

fought to keep out the independent suppliers of accessories throughout the decade. This is from a contemporary advertisement:

Everybody can dress up a Harley-Davidson.
Not everybody can do it right.

"Too many riders treat the purchase of a set of pipes or a sissy bar as though they were buying a star for the top of the Christmas tree. So long as it stays on, everything's fine.

Well, everything isn't so fine . . . You don't hang pipes on a Harley-Davidson. You fit them. Perfectly. So that they become part of the machine . . . Every Harley-Davidson accessory – from coolers to highway pegs to touring seats – is available at any Harley-Davidson dealer. So when you dress your Harley-Davidson motorcycle, you can dress it right . . . You've already committed yourself to riding one of the finest motorcycles the world has ever known . . . This is no time to start making compromises . . . Part of a motorcycle. Not parts on a motorcycle."

The sentiments of the advert would probably have been heartily endorsed by John E. Harley, Manager of Parts and Accessories and son of founder Bill, who lost the battle with cancer at the end of 1976. In true H-D fashion, the family tradition of service continued as his son, John E. Jnr, joined the company just one year earlier.

As previously mentioned, the Aermacchi/Harley Davidson concern came to an end in 1978, and after 30 years H-D gave up on lightweights altogether. It certainly wasn't the end of the Varese story however: today, Cagiva are among the most successful motorcycle manufacturers in Europe.

In 1979, the company built more than 50,000 V-twins when AMF took over ten years earlier, the production capacity across the board wasn't much more than 15,000. The anti-AMF feeling among Harley fans is partly to do with build quality. There is no doubt that the Italian lightweights were often poorly finished, and warranties were called in far too often on the York products as well. AMF had tried to do something that, in effect, was impossible: to mass-produce the big twins. The simple logistics of transporting the engines and transmissions from Capitol Drive to York militated against it. More importantly, the very design of the machines made it a doomed enterprise, no matter how many parts the company bought in from Japan – another, less justifiable reason to rail against the parent company. Even if AMF had succeeded in true mass-production (acknowledging that 50,000 V-twins in one year isn't exactly a cottage industry) it is doubtful that the subsequent reduction in costs and therefore price would have produced a mass market. Strange as it may seem, there are only a certain number of people who actually want a Harley-Davidson! (As for those warranty problems, well, for example, electrics were sometimes haywire on several models, finish was not always up to scratch on such expensive pieces of hardware, the old problem of oil leaks still hadn't gone away, piston rings broke too soon, there were many problems associated with AMF's attempt to maximize profits, and, of course, such problems can easily turn off a dealer if he's not given support from the supplier, which sometimes he wasn't.)

Another complaint sometimes heard is that AMF didn't put enough money into development, so that the Japanese were always one jump ahead. This is in part validated by the fact that nobody was waiting in the wings to snap up the company when AMF decided to bail out, fearful perhaps that a whole new range of motorcycles would have to be designed, with resultant massive tooling costs. But the Research and Development Department at Juneau Avenue had been active under AMF, looking at watercooling for example, and ohc V-twin layouts. More tangibly, there were new models for the first year of the new decade. They didn't come out of nowhere. Development work for the next generation engine, the next great leap forward for the Harley-Davidson marque, had begun early in the decade that fashion forgot. (Even the official H-D leathers managed to look decidedly unfunky).

"There's a kind of man who wears the Harley-Davidson brand. It burns deeper every time he swings into the saddle and lights the fire . . . That's the kind of man who'll get off on our new leathers."

Not sure what else he gets off on, but looking at the model in the advert, the list includes polo neck sweaters and Zapata moustaches.

BELOW: A 1979 Electra Glide, with S&S carb and filter.

Harley-Davidson
Classic

CHAPTER NINE

V2

Putting a Rocket under the Competition

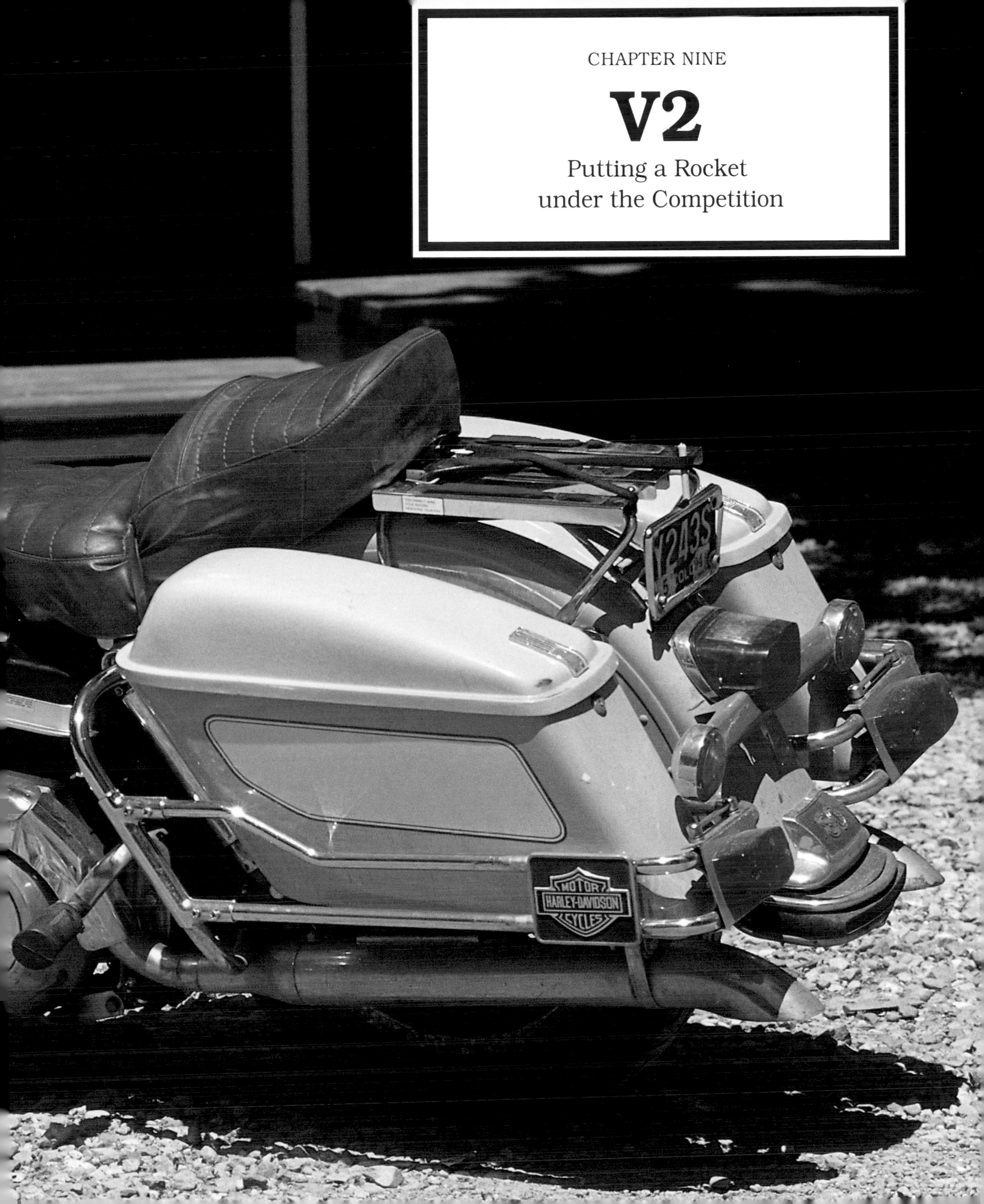

In 1980, Harley Davidson provided three – yes count them, three – brand new models. First of all, the major newcomer, the FLT Tour Glide. It was immediately recognizable because of the twin headlight fairing mounted on the frame, had five speeds for the first time on a V-twin, and steering geometry which improved handling significantly. The steering head was in front of the fork crowns. With the head lug behind, the effect was practically power steering, in comparison with the FLH which the FLT was intended eventually to replace. The uneven firing which is integral to the V-twin layout, as already pointed out, causes vibration at certain revs. Acknowledging the problem – it would be unfair to say for the first time – H-D set the engine up in such a way that it could flex in a longitudinal direction. Elastomer mounts intercepted vibrations to isolate the rider, one at the front of the engine, two at the rear of the gearbox. The new V-Fire ignition was another definitive advance. There were also triple disc brakes and an enclosed secondary chain. The fuel tank was bigger at five gallons and there was more ground clearance; the FLH tended to drag its muffler when leaning over with any seriousness. Perhaps the most important of these transformations was the five speed gearbox, as the FLH had always needed a greater choice of ratios. Fifth on the FLT could be used almost as overdrive. Bigger saddlebags and a top box were fitted as standard. It was still the old shovelhead engine of course, but this machine was a genuinely new model. The drivetrain was integral to the rest of the machine, unlike the constantly adapted FL series.

The Electra Glide Classic was offered in 1980, alongside the base-line Electra Glide. The Classic came in black or tan and "creme" with the 80 cu.in. engine as standard. You could still get a 74 cu.in. Electra Glide in 1980, but not in 1981. The extra cubic inches allowed the compression ratio to be reduced from 8:1 to 7.4:1, which meant that no-lead premium gas could be burned. Valve guides and seals were better and the alternator more powerful.

There were two Sportsters for 1980, the XLH and the XLS, though the excellent name "Sportster" was to disappear and "Roadster" would take its place. The XLS (basically an XLH with extended forks, making it a smaller FX Low Rider) was actually introduced in 1979 as was the XLH, (nicknamed the "Hugger") with optional shorter shocks and a lower seat.

Everyone's allowed to have a favorite, and this is it. With the possible exception of the 1936 Knucklehead EL, admired for historical reasons – and just about any H-D machine in production today – the 1980 Sturgis evokes a personal lust for ownership. There have been technically better Harley-Davidsons, though this machine had a lot going for it. It's the look, and this particular beholder sees only beauty. Vaughn Beals and the engineering depart-

PREVIOUS PAGES: The AMF era really hadn't been such a bad one: the company had continued to produce mighty engines like this Electra Glide Classic right up to the management buyout. But could the company be sustained without the massive AMF investment?

RIGHT: The distinctive FLT Tour Glide. With a newly designed frame, lighter steering and five gears, it was a big improvement on the old FLH.

Tour Glide
AVON

Harley-Davidson

STURGIS FXB 1980

The Sturgis returned to belt drive for the first time on an H-D machine since 1914.

Designations	n/a
Engine	ohv V-twin
Bore & stroke	3.50 × 4.25 in.
Displacement	80 cu. in.
Suspension	telescopic forks
Drive	primary and secondary belt drive
Top speed	106 mph

ment had returned to belts for primary and secondary drive on the FXB (B presumably for belt, not battery as for the FLHB) 80 cu.in. Sturgis: quieter, longer-lasting, but perhaps more importantly, another assault upon the age-old problem of engine vibration. It's black with orange trim – nature's way of telling you to step aside – and the engine completely dominates. It's low, with the seat 27 inches up, and has flat 'bars with risers. Top speed was around 106 mph. Electric start, but with a kick lever. No chain oiler of course. If you don't like it, seek professional help.

The third new machine for 1980, the Wide Glide, has already been described in the previous chapter. It is probably useful to look at the breakdown of models now available, and their relative numbers. The FLH is still there of course (for which read Electra Glide), with 80 and 1200 designations, even the 1979 anniversary Classic is still being built, but the standard FL has gone. Including police models, about 7500 of the FLH series were produced. Just 1470 FXB Sturgis cruisers were put together. About 4500 of the new FLT came down the line, the same for the Fat Bob FXEF 80, but a surprising 6000 Wide Glides, FXWG were produced and slightly fewer Low Riders. As to the "standard" Glide/Sportster hybrid the FXE (for electric), 3169 were manufactured. The Sportster (for which now read Roadster) twosome came in at 3000 for the XLS – remember, a long-forked low-slung version –

Sturgis

ABOVE: Custom-built enduro-style XLH Sportster built for the Alligator Enduro, pictured at Daytona in 1993.

PREVIOUS PAGES: The wonderful FXB shot against a suitable backdrop.

and a whopping 11,841 for the XLH. (All figures taken from David K. Wright's updated *The Harley-Davidson Motor Company: An Official Ninety-Year History.*)

It is difficult to draw hard-and-fast conclusions from the figures; the Sportsters seem to dominate, but obviously, there was a smaller profit margin on the less expensive machines. Let's just say that the spinoffs from the FX – the Wide Glide, the Fat Bob, the Low Rider, the Sturgis – were a very, very good idea. And the figures for 1981 show the FX series holding its ground, while the Glides and the Sportsters slipped back.

However the figures break down, they weren't attractive enough for AMF. On February 26, 1981, senior Harley-Davidson executives announced their intention to purchase the company. The deal was signed in June, steered through by Vaughn Beals, the AMF executive who had overseen H-D. Also among the purchasing group were Willie G. and company President, Charles Thompson. A ride was organized from York to Milwaukee to celebrate the event, under the banner "the eagle soars alone."

All the machines discussed above were still in production in 1981, except that the FLT had become the FLT Classic with crossover muffler system. The Heritage, a dressed up FLH 80 was offered, with fringed leather saddlebags and an old, suspended seat. Only a small number were made, but the machine is appropriately symbolic. It asks the question "What have the new owners actually inherited?" The answer, perhaps, was "A glorious history and not much else." It also looks forward to the nostalgia boom which H-D would exploit brilliantly.

It was more or less business as usual at the York and Milwaukee plants for that first year under new management. The problems that faced H-D were, however, massive. The umbrella of AMF money was no longer there, interest rates were soaring as worldwide inflation raged. The effects of the mid-1970s oil price hike were beginning to be felt. Japan had been overproducing motorcycles which were stockpiled across the US and being offered for sale at incredibly low prices. It is extremely fortunate that Vaughn Beals was an executive with the experience and vision to capitalize on

LEFT: 1990s Wide Glide; the Wide Glides, the Fat Bobs, the Super Glide II, all owe their existence to Willie G.'s first cruiser, the 1971 Super Glide.

BELOW: A barely recognizable 1987 FXSTC Custom Softail. Is that an Evo engine in there?

ABOVE: In some ways it's ridiculous to talk about entry level or female/inexperienced rider Harley-Davidson machines; they are all big, heavy chunks of metal, but their very size gives a degree of stability and (relative) safety, in comparison with the Japanese superbikes.

RIGHT: His'n'hers on the beach. The Hugger of 1987 was a blessing for some female H-D enthusiasts, but not all choose to ride Sportsters by any means.

what the company had – brand loyalty – and turn the situation around.

In 1982 the FXR Super Glide II was introduced, with 80 cu.in. (of course) and five-speed transmission. It would prove to be the first in a new series. It wasn't just a stripped FLT. It actually had a new frame, lighter than that of the Tour Glide but much, much stiffer. The front end looked FX-like, the overall feel was definitely Super Glide, and the press really liked it. The FXRS, in the same year, offered cast wheels, highway pegs, two-tone paint. The Sportsters, both XLH and XLS, also benefited hugely from a new frame, again lighter and stiffer, welded and stamped to avoid iron joints. The compression ratio dropped from 9:1 to 8:1 thanks to emission regs.

And once again, it got rave reviews, and the weight saving was substantial; but that didn't prevent a month-long plant shutdown to clear backlog in the same year, the loss of jobs, a freeze on management salaries and eventually a cut in production of 50 percent. The company lobbied for tariffs on motorcycle imports – as it had done as far back as 1951; the difference being that this time it won. A further 45 per cent tariff was levied on all machines over 700cc after the first 6000 units, reducing over five years. The British machines were exempted because their numbers were so few they did not merit protectionist assault; it was of course the Japanese imports which were the target. Also exempted were machines already in the USA, of which there was a fantastically high number.

There were two moves for 1983, one simple, not particularly interesting, marketing-led and successful, the other engineering-led, intriguing, and largely unsuccessful. The XLX-61, an absolutely base-line Sportster was offered at the cheapest price the company and dealers could withstand. It sold, and the further intriguing question is how many people stepped into the dealer's showroom to take a look, and signed up for an XLH, FLT, or (a dealer's dream) even an FXRT, the new Sport Glide with its anti-dive air-assisted suspension? Not many, but some.

So much for the come-on. Now the

ABOVE: An FXSTC Softail Custom, this one from 1989.

OPPOSITE: The XR 1000 certainly was an impressive looking beast, even if production was short. This one has the race kit for 100 bhp performance.

engineering. The XR 750 had dominated AMA dirt track in the 1970s and there had been requests for a production model. The racing department gave it a shot. The 1972 XR 750 engine had alloy heads and these were retained, mated to iron barrels and the lower end of the XL 1000 engine. With a lot of effort, the powerplant was made to fit in the XL frame, and was, in fact, put into the XLX base model. In retrospect, the much higher cost of this limited edition didn't square with the basis XLX package. 70 bhp and a potential approaching 100 bhp with speed kit for the XR 1000, 11½ in. discs front and rear, dual Dell'Orto carbs, plus Jay Springsteen's victory at Daytona Battle of the Twins on the machine that year, weren't quite enough to convince the potential customers. Production ceased in 1984.

Another offering for 1983 was the FLHT, the FLT frame but with the new five speeds and the elastomer anti-vibration three-point isolation of the engine from the backside.

Harley-Davidsons had been threatening for years to get tough with those who used its name without permission; there were literally hundreds of aftermarket accessories and novelties outfits out there at the beginning of the 1980s doing just that. While everything had been up in the air during the AMF changeover, little had been done, but a 50 percent cut in production, and personal commitment to a company no longer sheltered by a larger conglomerate, focused the corporate mind. Threatening letters went out, and some were forced to pay up in court. H-D are still zealous in this regard: in 1993 a part-time Harley-Davidson restorer/tuner and full-time Harley-Davidson fanatic of my acquaintance was ordered to take down a hand-painted shield he had hanging outside his tiny back street garage. The company are right to protect their main asset – their name – even if the latter example was a little harsh. Again in 1993, the first model of a Harley-Davidson was produced by the Franklin Mint, a company which produces ceramic and die-cast models. Naturally, they are doing it under license from H-D. The point is not that they would try to get away without paying a percentage; rather, they would not bother to produce the model at all if the image was not guarded by its owner.

Rumors were flying in 1983 concerning new products from York. Vaughn Beals and the rest of the management team had rationalized the lines at the plants, attempting to reduce inventory in particular: stock

THIS PAGE: Customized license plates are one way of having fun with your machine, which is frowned upon across Europe.

is a killer at times of high inflation, and H-D were buying many parts in of necessity. The old system had been to buy in bulk to ensure that production numbers were kept up, with no delays waiting for parts from outside suppliers. But it made no sense to worry about keeping the line moving if the company was only working at half capacity anyway. Far better to free up the capital lying unused in all those foreign forks and carbs. The new management also sold off the golf-cart operation to concentrate on the core business.

One of the uses the money could be put to was in the engineering department, and

Harley-Davidson

XR 1000 1983

Offered with standard XLX frame and trim, the Special proved too expensive to attract enough sales.

Designations	n/a
Engine	ohv V-twin
Bore & stroke	3.189 × 3.812 in.
Displacement	1000 cc
Torque	71.4 ft/lbs @ 5600 rpm
BHP	70 stock, approaching 100 with race kit
Top speed	165 mph (racing)

some of it was. The department's membership grew, and a high percentage of H-D money was invested in development. Some of its money had been invested in this way over the previous six or seven years, to produce the most important Harley-Davidson change from 1984 to the present day.

It was clear that the shovelhead engine had been overtaken by technological refinement. The Japanese had entered the big bike market with a vengeance. The Honda GoldWing had been released in 1975 as a flat four with shaft drive and water cooling. It had grown from 1000cc to 1100cc in 1981, then 1200cc for 1984. Still to come, in 1987, was the gigantic (798 lb) 1500cc six cylinder Aspencade. Yamaha had shown off its very first V-twins to American dealers prior to the 1981 season. The sohc 750cc Virago and the XV920 had the cylinders at 75 degrees, leaving just enough room to tuck the carburetors neatly away in the V. Unlike Harley-Davidson, Yamaha didn't have the baggage of 80 years of history with them and could choose the angle, rather than have it dictated to them by an ancient need to marry two single cylinders and tuck them in a

bicycle frame. The Virago was pure H-D custom in style.

The loyalty of the Harley-Davidson faithful was the cornerstone of survival, as demand for larger machines waned and the competition multiplied. As part of the drive to involve the customer with the company, alongside promotions such as the annual exhibition at the Daytona Hilton in Bike Week, publicity rides and rallies, the Harley Owner's Group was formed in 1983. $30 pa, the first year free when you bought your machine. There were 100,000 members by the end of the decade. 1983 was also the year when the V2 Evolution engine was announced, to be fitted across the range on five models for 1984.

Before looking at the technical details, what were the real options and the requirements for a new generation of Harley-Davidson motorcycles? Firstly, the lightweight and middleweight effort had ceased. H-D made big bikes, and were known for making big bikes. Secondly, there was a market for such machines: the mere fact that Honda had entered the arena after careful consideration proved it. Thirdly, H-D

BELOW: **The FXRT, with the anti-dive forks first seen on the FXRS; purposeful, and neat.**

LEFT: FLHTC Ultra Classic Tour Glide, 1989, the first production year for the Electra Glide Ultra Classic, as well.

ABOVE: The beautiful cap on Richard Johnson's Ultra Classic Tour Glide.

were not just associated with big machines, but V-twins specifically. Fourth and very important, the buyers of Harley-Davidson's product were not really looking for out-and-out performance or leading-edge technology, nor was the company capable of producing one of the dozens of transverse four-cylinder four-stroke Japanese street machines, or, for example the mid-eighties Honda V4 VFR750. Perhaps it is unfair to say that they were not actually capable of producing such machines; the large engineering department probably was, given enough time and money, (and there was talk of 500cc and upwards, shaft drive, liquid-cooled machinery being prepared with German input), but to do so would have meant risking the dilution of the big V-twin company image.

The only option then, was V-twin, but better; and that is exactly what the V2 engine provided. The shovelhead continued in production alongside the V2 in 1984, notably in the FLH Electra Glide Classic. Despite the fact that the V2 was undoubtedly a better engine, H-D retained the shovelhead, partly to use up stock, and partly to avoid alienating Glide lovers.

The V2 Evolution motor was a 45-degree V-twin. It was based initially on the shovelhead bottom and – another fact that doesn't exactly rock you back on your heels – with 80 in. cases. It was a classic H-D update, not a back-to-the-drawing-board (or in this case, to the computer) connecting-rods-outward revolution. But the improvements made in just about every department definitely add up to a new powerplant. The alloy cylinder barrels with iron liners were far more efficient in getting rid of the heat. The engine was lighter, more powerful, easier to maintain and cleaner. The heads were attached to the crankcases with straight-through bolts to firm everything up and avoid heat distortion, the domed pistons were replaced with flat Mahle pistons, the combustion chamber was a different, more efficient shape, the valve gear was modified, and the electronic firing was super-efficient.

Several machines benefited from the new technology. The FLT/FLHT/FLHTC, the "H", as described earlier, acquired five speeds and the new engine mounts; the "C" meant some extra bits and bobs. The machines not only received the new engine, they also had the "anti-dive" forks as first

ABOVE: They don't come much more radically customized than this fabulous FXSTC Softail.

seen on the FXRS. They were not restyled, it was just the timing case proudly announcing "V2". Mid-way through the year, a cunning new clutch was added, with lubricated clutch plates that demanded less effort from the rider when changing gears.

The FXRS/FXRT Glides were also V2-powered and also had the new clutch. There was a limited edition FXRDG, the Disc Glide, with a solid black back wheel and fancy paint. The new engine cruised at 60 or 70 without overheating.

The new look for 1984, the true beginnings of the "New Nostalgia" – Willie G.'s phrase, I believe – was the FXST Softail. Basically a Wide Glide but with the V2 engine, the difference was in the rear suspension. The springs and gas-assisted horizontally-mounted shocks were tucked away under the gearbox. The swing arm masqueraded as the old rigid rear section, with the pivot disguised by the seat. This was done for one reason and one reason only: to evoke hardtail nostalgia. It's an example of form not following function, but getting away with it. The engineers had a choice of five gear transmission or kick start – there wasn't room for both – and they chose, quite logically, the kick. Part and parcel, after all, of the retro look. The overall impression – clean lines, the engine, of course, gleaming and completely open, not obscured under fiberglass, the mock hardtail – was reminiscent of fifties choppers. The machine was the best H-D seller in 1984

Harley-Davidson

SOFTAIL FXST 1989

Engine	ohv V^2
Bore & stroke	3.498 × 4.250 in.
Displacement	1340 cc
Compression ratio	8.5:1
Torque	80 ft/lbs @ 4000 rpm
Wheelbase	66.3 in.

and 1985. In fact, the FX machines were way ahead of the big tourers, in which market the GoldWing had made serious inroads. Built in the States, it circumvented the import tariffs.

In 1985 FX and FT machines were fitted with belt secondary drive. There was something missing, still, from the lineup; there was room for a machine that would come in lighter than the Sportsters, while not directly competing with the Japanese middleweights in performance. Such a machine would be a fine entry-level introduction for those who were not already in the H-D saddle. The V2 80 cu.in. work had been done. The challenge was now to replicate all that was good about the new engine, with a smaller capacity. The result was the 1986 V2 Evolution 883. Flat-topped pistons and alloy cylinder heads as on the V2 80, the new wet clutch, Computer Aided Design camshaft, hydraulic valve lifters as on the bigger twins, and a modified oil system helped to increase service intervals. Only four speeds – not enough room for a fifth; that wouldn't be figured out until 1991.

What did the new Sportster look like? Well, it was low, the tank was small, it was an XLX frame. It looked like a Harley-Davidson; that is, unlike any of the competition with a similar capacity. Very shortly afterwards, in the same year, an 1100cc version was also ready. Big brother was rated at 63 bhp, its sibling at 53, with 1200 to come.

The company wasn't out of the financial woods yet; in fact, as a manufacturing-intensive producer of expensive leisure equipment, it probably never can be wholly secure. The start-up costs for a new machine that might not find favor are phenomenal. In June 1986 one of the banks got cold feet and the company had to issue shares again, selling enough stock to round up sufficient cash to refinance and carry on

BELOW: 1991 FLSTC; the 1936 graphics suit the machine very well.

Harley-Davidson

HERITAGE SOFTAIL CLASSIC FLSTC 1989

Engine	ohv V^2
Bore & stroke	3.498 × 4.250 in.
Displacement	1340 cc
Compression ratio	8.5:1
Torque	80 ft/lbs @ 4000 rpm
Wheelbase	62.7 in.

ABOVE: 1989 XL Hugger, again, with some radical paint and chrome.

the good work. Another circumstance not quite beyond H-D's control were federal noise limitation statutes: all machines had a new exhaust for 1986.

The FL Softail had a makeover for 1986, to become the Heritage Softail Classic, FLSTC, with studded two-piece seat, windshield, leather saddlebags, wire wheels, footboards and an enclosed FL-looking fork. Going in the opposite direction, in 1987 the FLHS Electra Glide Sport became a little lighter in standard trim, with more responsive handling and front and rear crash bars. It's changes like this which lead to the blasphemous comment "all Harleys look alike to me." 1987 was also the 30th anniversary of the Sportster, and never a company to let a birthday pass without a party, the Evo Sportster got some more chrome and the black engine of the FL machines, plus of course, a special paint scheme – orange and black – the same colors as the 1980 Sturgis, but how could you follow that masterpiece? Similarly, the FXLR Low Rider's tenth anniversary present was its own high bars.

Remember Vaughn Beals and Willie G. riding off to meet their public and gladhand their dealers for the 75th anniversary? Mr Beals had an even better PR promotion for 1978. The import tariff set in 1984 had been intended to run for five years; H-D requested that it be rescinded. As any snake oil salesman will tell you, selling is all about confidence, and here was a clear message to the world: our house is in order and we are ready to take on all-comers. At that time, there was a strong protectionist feeling in the USA, being resisted by President Reagan. Almost at the same moment, Richard Teerlink, who had done so much to keep the company in business as its Chief Finance Officer, became the company President. The company had diversified again, buying the Indiana-based Holiday Rambler Corporation, which made motor homes.

Also in 1987, the Hugger, a lowered version of the 883 Sportster, was introduced, for those little guys whose feet couldn't reach the asphalt and, according to the company itself, for female riders.

In 1988, larger carburetors improved performance, and in a typical piece of retro styling, the FXRS Low Rider had a built-in fuel gauge on the tank, as it had in 1977. The forks got fatter on the Sportsters and the

1987-88 FXRs. More retro: the FXST Springer Softail appeared with fake forties-style sprung forks. A Springer at the time of writing will cost you around £10,300 ($15,450) in the UK, which may come as something of a shock to those fortunate enough to live and ride in the USA. The Heritage Softail Classic is not much more, the Heritage Softail Nostalgia is around £11,200 ($16,800) and the Ultra Classic Electra Glide is a few pennies short of £12,800 ($19,200). If you're going to upgrade from the Ultra, stop drinking and start saving for a Bimota YB10 Biposto at £18,000 ($27,000) – there's nowhere else to go.

The Sportster gained 12 per cent more horsepower in 1988 (according to the company) upgrading from 1987 1100 cc to 1200 cc. 1988 is of course another H-D anniversary; 85 years in business was marked by some graphics and, more importantly, by the FXSTS Springer Softail, harking back to pre-telescopic times. 1989 was the first year for the Ultra Classics. The Electra Glide Ultra Classic and the Tour Glide both had cruise control, built-in CB, and an 80-watt four-speaker stereo.

LEFT: Springer Softail forks, another gesture toward the "New Nostalgia" for 1988.

BELOW: Special edition Dyna Glide, marking the 50th anniversary of Daytona.

More or less the final important change to the H-D lineup to the present day – and that of course is tempting fate, in the company's 90th year – began with the 1991 FXDB Sturgis. This was a limited edition (1700) machine which featured the Dyna Glide frame. It was black, and it was long. The forks were 33-inch, 32-degree rake. These, the 'bar risers, the extra inch on the swinging arm and the somewhat inadequate three inches of travel for the rear wheel were all designed to stretch the image. Despite the harsh ride, the look found enough favor for the FXDB Daytona to be produced in celebration of the fiftieth anniversary of Daytona Raceweek. The Dyna Glide chassis was set off by some blue and gold pearlglo

Harley-Davidson

FLHR ELECTRA GLIDE ROAD KING 1994

The latest Electra Glide, characterized by angular integral panniers and dual headlamps.

Designations	n/a
Engine	(40mm Mikuni carb) ohv V^2
Bore & stroke	3.50 × 4.25 in.
Displacement	80 cu.in.
Compression ratio	8.5:1
Dry weight	314 kg

LEFT: A Heritage Softail out for a run with one of its cousins, the Lowrider.

paint, and dual disc brakes were an attempt to answer what is probably the most repeated complaint about H-D machinery, (particularly the big tourers), that moving is fine, but stopping is a long, drawn-out process. This was also a limited edition machine, but in the following year (1992) the Dyna Glide made it into full production with the FXDC Dyna Glide Custom. The Dyna Glide chassis wasn't just designed for looks: there would be little point in spending so much money to produce machines that are very close to the FXR series already available, in terms of function. The new machines had to look like the old 1970s Low Riders, but with handling and ride at least as good as the Evo FXRs. The single backbone chassis, the forgings at frame junctions and the engine isolation mountings, were designed to do just that.

In 1990, the Heritage Softail spawned what is really quite an outrageous looking machine; outrageous, that is, if compared to any machines in the same price bracket from other manufacturers. Compare the Harley-Davidson Fat Boy with, say, a BMW K1100LT, or a 1992 Yamaha GTS1000 with its Omega chassis, electronic fuel injection and ABS. Look (probably blankly) at the Japanese machine's single-sided swinging arm front suspension and then take in the metallic silver, flared steel front fender atop the cast disc wheel of the Harley. Are we in the same decade? Are we in the same business. Yes to the first, not altogether to the second. The FLSTF Fat Boy is another prime example of the ongoing H-D theme: solidity, product recognition, plenty of steel. So the Yamaha has mysteriously effective anti-dive handling, computer-designed haute couture: so what? The "Fat Boy" tag says it all: this is *not* a performance motorcycle, unless by performance you mean touring at low revs and taking in the scenery. The yellow headlights on the chrome engine, the shotgun pipes, the pigskin seat, are all part of the pleasure. It remains to be seen if, (for slightly more money) the GTS1000 will seduce more riders than its very, very distant American cousin. What is certain is that nobody will be *converted* either way. The Japanese machine was actually designed as a sports/tourer, with its ergonomically designed fairing, so it should in theory be battling for the same market (or perhaps more accurately for the FXR market). But no H-D owner would countenance owning one, just as those who sneer at the retro movement and love tomorrow's toys wouldn't be seen dead on the H-D lump.

Where does that leave us? It leaves us with XLH 883, XLH 833 Hugger and XLH 1200; Super Glide, Low Rider Sport, Low Rider Custom, Low Rider Convertible, Electra Glide Sport and Dyna Low Rider; Softail Custom, Springer Softail, Heritage Softail Classic and Heritage Softail Nostalgia; Fat Boy, Dyna Wide Glide, Electra Glide Classic and Ultra Classic Electra Glide. That's the lineup at the time of writing: that is, the XLH Sportsters, the FXR series, the FX (and FL) Softails, and the FL Kings of the Highway. You should be able to pick out the basics of these four strands, even though a few have not yet been mentioned. It's the FX series that has allowed for the most factory custom treatments over the years. Pay a little more than you would for the FXR Super Glide, and your Low Rider will have a black and silver engine, forward-mounted pegs, tank-mounted speedo and tachometer. Alternatively, the FXLR Custom will get you pullbacks, a laced front wheel and a cast disc at the rear. The Convertible you should be able to guess: correct, detachable windshield and saddlebags as standard. The Sport has "sports suspension", gas-assisted adjustable front and rear shocks, and a different front profile more suited to cutting through the air, rather than sauntering through it in a leisurely manner on the Convertible.

BELOW: **FLSTF: that's F for Fat! Shotgun pipes standard.**

Since the introduction of the Dyna Glides and the Fat Boy, refinement of the existing machinery has been the aim. In 1992, the whole lineup was improved with new brake disc and pad material, which took some of the sweat out of slowing down. Fasteners all received an extra anti-corrosion treatment – which of course is tantamount to an admission of guilt – and an extra clear lacquer top coat, baked-on powder, is on all the machines post-1992. For the Sportsters, the major change was the 1991 rethink for five speeds and belt drive option. It's difficult to imagine much more being done to the "baby" Harleys, except a constant attempt to improve finish and build quality. The 1340 Evo engines in the rest of the range have been recalibrated to help cold starting and the oil filter was relocated to the front of the crankcase. The steel oil lines were new for 1992, as was the redesigned oil pump cover. It's somehow gratifying to see H-D still grappling with one of the integral problems of the V-twin configuration: where to put the bits and pieces for lubrication. The FL models all now have gas-adjustable anti-dive front suspension, foot boards, and integral panniers with improved weather-proof seals.

Harley-Davidson have worked hard to protect their market position against their rivals simply by producing outstanding bikes. A perfect example is the 1994 Road King, a special 90th anniversary celebration of the mythical Electra Glide series, with distinctive integral panniers, about 30 square feet of chrome, windscreen and special dual headlamps. Nobody could create this beauty without the groundwork of nigh-on 30 years of Electra Glides already in place. You simply can't tool up from scratch for such a machine, even if you have billions of yen to play with: the risk is too great. Dry weight for the machine is 314 kg, primary transmission Duplex chain, secondary belt, Fat Bob tank, elastomer-mounted 1340 cc V-twin, everything sounds familiar. 290 mm double discs at the front, single at the back. The machine is certainly worthy of its proud ancestry, as is the 1994 FXDS Dyna Low Rider, the Convertible. Same engine, same brakes as the Road King, lighter of course at 281 kg; and a different inclination of the forks and improved suspension in comparison with 1993. Leather saddlebags and plexiglass windscreen as standard. Perhaps the most beautiful machine for 1994 is the straight retro FLSTN Heritage Softail Nostalgia special, with its whitewall tires and Fat Boy-type fenders. The bike's classic lines are enhanced by wonderful pearl gray and white paint with red pinstriping.

As has been stressed already, one of the greatest marketing successes of Harley-Davidson has been its insistent, sometimes subtle, sometimes relentless invitation to all riders to individualize their machines with aftermarket accessories. You could argue

that the FXR range, in particular, is simply starting the job for you, though there are in fact some genuine technical characteristics specific to each model. The pictures in this book tell the customizing story, one which goes far beyond the official chrome axle nut covers (or the *Easyriders* official doggie sunglasses, come to that). One favorite example then, of how people just won't leave well alone – and produce something wonderful in the process. Craig's Heritage Softail was featured in the November/December 1993 *All American Heroes*, one of the myriad magazines devoted to the American icon. It looks superb: blue paint, the seat has been replaced with something less obtrusive, the mudguards are minimalist. The running gear is all stock. The major transformation is that the machine has a rigid frame supplied by Cobra Engineering in the U.K. Why describe this machine, rather than some extraordinary work of art by Arlen Ness, or some Nitro tire stripper? Well, what was the point of the Softails? To imitate the old-style hardtails, but by sleight of hand to provide modern rear suspension. What this owner has done is to take a machine that was specifically designed to *pretend* to be a hardtail – and made it one! Iron irony at its best. Long may the desire to take a stock machine, and graft an identity on to it, burn in the hearts of Harley-Davidson riders everywhere. That desire has produced one of the greatest sideshows in history.

ABOVE: A radical 1993 XCH 1200 Sportster. If you want to get into customizing from a standing start, you'll have to start learning the language. Start off by defining triple trees, widowmakers and goosenecking.

CHAPTER TEN

THE LOOK THAT MEANS AMERICAN

LIVE TO RIDE
RIDE TO LIVE
EAGLE-SPIRIT

If you want to know just how Harley-Davidson would like you to see their machines, all you have to do, of course, is look at their advertising copy year after year. "The look that *means* American" is copy from an early 1980s advertisement, though you would have to read on and identify Wide Glide, Low Rider and Roadster to know it wasn't from the 1950s. You see "the look . . . in all our gas tanks, from the original teardrop Peanut to Fat Bob. You feel it with our pullback buckhorn handlebars, low stepped seats with sissy bars and the unique Harley riding position. And chrome is where it belongs: on the hardware and the staggered shorty duals." There is plenty of information about custom paint, but nothing about the aforementioned "hardware", except that it's chromed – remember that this is pre-V2. There are no performance stats, no top speeds, no mpg, certainly no price guides – but that's the way with most motorcycle manufacturers – no differentiation among the machines except in terms of styling, and (hardly surprising) no mention in the 1980 AMF advertisement of the imminent withdrawal of the parent company.

The phrase "more than a machine" is repeated. Contrast this approach with, say, BMW, where the thrust of the argument is that the product is very much a machine: here is the package, the new "erogonomically designed" R1100 RS, for example, with its "second generation ABS"; incidentally, BMW make a big thing about how recyclable and environmentally friendly the machine is, another strong contrast with most H-D advertising. The German marque will use the slogan *Freude am Fahren*, "joy of driving" (more accurately for the autos than for the bikes, of course), but it will also bombard you with technical information, rather than appealing to an enthusiasm for all things Bavarian. If there is a technical advance, H-D will certainly let you know about it – viz the Hydra-Glide and the Evo – and will sometimes provide full specifications, but for most of the time the approach is the same. The company understood at a remarkably early stage that it was, indeed, offering "more than a machine." This in 1927, for the 74: "refined in many details – but no radical departures from the time-tried Harley-Davidson design." And in 1974: "Pleasant dreams. You're big enough to do all those neat things you've been dreaming about on a Harley-Davidson X-90 . . . The Great American Freedom Machine." Freedom and dreams; not CAD-CAM frame design.

This is where things get a little delicate. How many times have people tried to explain the enduring fascination with Harley-Davidson by pointing out that the company is "as American as apple pie", or that love of the V-twins is part of an American love of all things big, allied to the love of Cadillacs, or big-finned Chevys, the same spirit that built the Empire State Building and the Hoover Dam? The company has certainly striven to

PREVIOUS PAGES: Evo engine on a 1989 FXSTC Softail Custom. The V2 was a classic example of careful Harley-Davidson development; the old shovelhead had remained in production alongside the new engine for the first year.

RIGHT: "Live to ride, ride to live," Harley-Davidson big V-twins in their element, with sun, sky and two-lane blacktop.

RIGHT: **Milwaukee iron; made in America, chromed in the Crab Nebula. Individuation is the essential element in today's Harley-Davidson success story.**

associate its product with this kind of amorphous, pioneering tradition and at several periods in its history the appeal to patriotism was quite direct, particularly during the British bike invasion of the 1950s and again when Japanese machines began to bite into the H-D market. But the fact that the marketeers *wanted* motorcyclists to think this way about H-D doesn't necessarily mean that this is the reason so many remain loyal to Milwaukee for a lifetime. On another, even more unsatisfactory tack, some have read ''Amateur Psychologist's Weekly'' and decided it's all to do with machismo. Just about any attempt to explain commitment to Harley-Davidson is destined to annoy, if not send into paroxyms of fury and denial, those who actually ride the machines.

There are two reasons: one is that most of the theories are hogwash, if the pun can be excused. The second is that the experience of owning and riding a Harley-Davidson is a very personal, idiosyncratic one, despite the obvious expression of belonging to a very special club in evidence at meets, both official and unofficial. The opportunity to individualize your machine, so fervently encouraged by the company for sound economic reasons, is taken up and expresses outwardly the particular aspirations of the rider. One theory, therefore, is not going to explain why an 18-year-old in London dreams of nothing but a stripped Sportster with Screamin' Eagle Evolution XL bolt-on hydraulic cams, while a 50-year-old Hou-Tex HOG chapter member anxiously checks his FLHT Electra Glide for signs of stress after every Sunday run. The experience is different.

Far better not to attempt to explain the phenomenon at all, but that would be cheating. "Cult" is an unattractive word, so let's say that the Harley culture obviously exists, from the tattoos to the magazines, from the Vietnam Vets MC to the outlaws. *Some* kind of comment is required, even it it's hedged round with expressions of uncertainty.

LEFT: Even the bear looks like what the British, back in the fifties, used to call a "greaser."

BELOW: A Softail, in this case, straight out of the crate, as the factory intended it should look, and no fancy paint.

OPPOSITE, ABOVE: Clark Gable was a big man, but there was plenty of room to tuck in those size 15 feet on a Harley, back in the 1940s.

RIGHT: Some superb decoration on a Wide Glide.

So, first, the look of the thing. Oscar Wilde said that every man should either create a work of art, or be one. Billionaire Malcolm Forbes could have told him there was a third way: buy one. He bought 50 Harley-Davidsons, so he obviously wasn't buying something just to get to the office on. He was buying on aesthetic grounds: he liked having Harleys around. It would take an expert in the plastic arts, or at the very least a brilliant designer, to explain just why the proportions of most Harley-Davidsons look right, and I am neither. Suffice to say, the engine is always the star of the show, not hidden by steel or fiberglass as is sometimes the case on other makes, and it seems to dictate the lines of the machine. The Yamaha lookalikes don't really look alike. It would be worth measuring one in minute detail to discover the precise differences: maybe an air cleaner a few millimetres smaller, or a whisker more length on the forks, would make all the difference. Even if you can't tell the difference without looking for the badges, just as with any work of art, you prefer the original to the copy anyway. (Though the 75 degrees between the cylinders make it obvious from the start.)

RIGHT: A sight to strike terror, or prompt idle curiosity? Hell's Angels, 1966.

Harley culture relies upon instant product recognition, which has been protected and nurtured down the years. In the words of US rep W. D. Vandiver, "Frothy eloquence neither convinces nor satisfies me. I am from Missouri. You have got to show me." The flathead, the panhead, the knucklehead, the shovelhead, the V2, do just that. The engine tells you what you are looking at.

Secondly, the Harley-Davidson sect is very ecumenical, non-exclusive. In New York, 70 per cent of new buyers are college graduates. The average age of a new H-D customer is now just under 40. If Harley-Davidson had been indelibly marked as part of youth culture, it would have been too embarassing for the "rubbies' – the rich urban bikers – to have taken the plunge. Similarly, if the marque had been tainted, rather than pleasantly colored, by outlaw associations, there would be no sale to the doctors and lawyers. At the same time, the "rubby" element makes no difference to the backstreet tuner, the weekend racer or the Sonny Barger aspirant.

The Italian importers of H-D described

ABOVE: Big bikes in not-so-little Tokyo. H-D riders gather in Japan in 1992 to demonstrate for a better deal for riders.

the 1993 sales figures as "un miracolo," and felt they could expand quicker than Fiat. In the same year, "nerissimo" was the word that Kawasaki Italia used to describe the motorcycle market as a whole: which means awful black. Apart from the Harley-Davidson look, and the ability of the H-D fraternity to absorb all saints and sinners, what else helps to explain such confidence and such universal recognition of Harley culture? The advertising itself of course, together with the free advertising of magazines and books, has been important. *The Enthusiast* magazine was launched under the auspices of the company in 1916, as part of the attempt to bind not just owners but dealers more closely to the company: at the same time, Arthur Davidson set up a network of factory representatives across the country to liaise with the dealers – and keep and eye on them.

But a distinction must be drawn between the literature the company can influence or control, and the opinions it can't. It is only in recent years – post-Evo approximately – that the established motorcycle magazines have got out of the habit of criticizing, sometimes deriding, H-D machines more or less as a matter of course, especially in Europe. The building of the myth has nevertheless been relentless by the company, and the success of so many periodicals exclusively devoted to the marque – not all approved of by the company – is in part explained very simply: no other motorcycle has so many variants. Customizing is endless, and therefore continuously photographically interesting, week in week out. The argument chases its own tail in the end – there are more machines in the Suzuki catalog, which should allow for variety, but not many would buy the monthly magazine, not even the owners. Harley-Davidson is fêted in the press because there is a Harley culture: the Harley culture is fed by the press.

The Portland, Oregon police have secured the services of a pig for sniffing out drugs: what's his name? Harley of course. The amazing thing is not that the name was chosen, but that vast numbers of people across the globe would know *why* it was chosen. There really are not that many Harley-Davidsons in the world, just as there aren't that many motorcyclists. But the eagle soars way beyond the factory, the dealerships, the race track, or the highway.

The fortunate owners of the latest machines will not be paying chicken feed for such steeds; will their enjoyment be more or less than Englishman Nigel Mills' experience of the Harley phenomenon? Maybe it's a funny way to end this attempt to define and explain the Harley-Davidson feel, but it's a reminder that the H-D phenomenon takes many different forms for many different people.

"I became the proud owner of a Harley-Davidson by accident – literally. My much prized Yamaha MX175DT trials bike had been rendered *hors de combat* after an argument with a Ford Cortina Mk 3, so the search began for a replacement. As I scanned the small ads my eyes fell on a 1976 Harley-Davidson SR 90, "£75 ono." The fierce English winter of 1978 was lashing the Derbyshire Peak District as I traveled to Dronfield Woodhouse to view the machine. It had been stored in the open for two years, protected by a tarpaulin. Brushing away a mound of snow before uncovering the bike, an initial inspection revealed two flat tires and seized brakes. But the black paintwork gleamed, and the rubber seals on the front forks were unbroken, the chrome being perfect with no pitting. Other than a bit of rust here and there (mostly on the swinging arm), the finish was surprisingly good. Encouragingly, after charging the battery the bike started first kick. I parted with £25 in cash (I had to haggle!) and the deal was done.

I brought the bike back to my father's garage for a complete strip-down and a thorough examination. The brakes were in

BELOW: Electra Glide Classic with full touring kit: lexan windshield, panniers and a little something extra at the back which will strain that high torque engine not one bit.

ABOVE: *Electra Glide in Blue* helped to formulate the Harley myth. When the man gets shot off his machine at the end of the movie, his trusty steed seems to roll on forever.

RIGHT: The King with the contemporary King of the Highway, the Duo-Glide.

poor condition, although the drums had not corroded despite the fact that the linings had come adrift due to dampness. After being professionally relined, the brakes were refitted and proved to be more than satisfactory. The SR 90's paintwork was enhanced (especially around the handsome black fuel tank), and the chrome was cleansed. Reassembled, the little H-D looked a million dollars and easily passed its MoT test for road-worthiness. The SR 90 was easy to ride, but could be skittish when cornering, due, no doubt, to its light weight and high center of gravity when compared to many contemporary machines. The bike certainly looked distinctive; its road-type bars, tank, seat and tires were combined with a high sump, giving the ground clearance of a trials iron.

Totally reliable, never failing to start despite temperatures down to −12°C, the SR 90 did, however, exhibit one alarming characteristic. The front pipe from the exhaust manifold was held in place by two springs, which were push-fitted into the baffle. If the bike had been left standing in very cold weather, a build-up of condensation in the front pipe resulted in an ear-splitting crack when the engine fired, the said front pipe flying off like a primitive anti-tank rocket some 15 yards down the road. Sometimes, angry pedestrians had to be mollified prior to the rider deftly refitting the pipe with a pair of pliers. The only other fault worth mentioning is that the engine cut dead the instant the main fuel tank emptied, there being no warning splutterings. But switching to the reserve and dipping the clutch quickly brought the bike back to life.

It wasn't long before the SR 90 attractd

MCB
FXRS

peer group admiration, and, while I was drinking in The Greenacres pub one evening, a collector offered me £300 for it, cash in hand, there and then. Technically, the bike was owned by my father, so I respectfully declined but promised to return the following evening with the word. The word turned out to be "no" because, tragically, the bike was stolen the very next day. Not by a rival enthusiast (true bikers don't steal), but by a mindless vandal, who, after abandoning it, decided to trash the SR 90, with bricks and a sledgehammer. The police reported that the cylinder head had been knocked clean off, the crankcase shattered, the frame bent, and the gas tank smashed beyond recognition. Needless to say, I was too upset to recover the wreck. I felt even more aggrieved when the collector who had wanted to buy the bike told me that he would have gladly paid up to £400 for it (the insurance company finally coughed up £125), and that it was one of only 12 Italian-made (Aermacchi) Harley-Davidson SR 90s imported into the UK. I later bought a brand new Honda CBX500, but it just wasn't the same."

Of course, it wasn't.

So what does the future hold for Harley-Davidson?

At the Daytona amateur races in March

OPPOSITE: Mickey Rourke and Don Johnson, in *Harley-Davidson and Malboro' Man.*

BELOW: The most famous of them all: Dennis Hopper and Peter Fonda in *Easy Rider.* Peter Fonda continues to glamorize the Harley image, 25 years on.

1994, former 500 Grand Prix rider Miguel DuHamel fought through the pack from outside the top ten to make it to the podium twice on a VR1000. The Harley-Davidson success, battling on even terms with Suzuki, Ducati and Kawasaki, caused a few raised eyebrows. The two third places were only in the amateur races of course, but perhaps they pointed toward the future for H-D. Experiments with water cooling are

ABOVE: Evel Knievel was wheeled in to help boost flagging sales in the early 1970s. He used XRs to make jumps, but his usefulness to H-D was tarnished somewhat after his altercation (involving a baseball bat) with an ex-business partner who had written a less than flattering book about the Montana legend.

still under wraps at the time of writing; truth to tell, it's just about impossible to predict the direction the company will take, but it's fun taking a guess. In the medium term, Harley-Davidson won't be challenging the likes of Honda's ready-to-race RC45, with its Programed Fuel Injection System (PGM-FI), 160mph and £18,000 ($27,000) price tag. How about BMW's new single cylinder sportster, their first truly sporting machine since the 1973 R90S, pencilled in for 1996? It's unlikely that H-D will enter that market – but they just might. One thing's for sure: there will still be big V-twins for celebrities to sit on as far ahead as anyone can see.

"We do not make something because the demand, the market, is there. With our technology we can create demand, we can create the market. Supply creates its own

BELOW: 19 cars cleared in 1971 before the start of the Miller 500 stock car race at Ontario Motor Speedway, the Harley-Davidson name nice and clear. Pity he couldn't do it on an FLH. Now that really would have been something . . .

LEFT: Arnie just had to be associated with heavy iron, here in *Terminator 2: Judgment Day*

RIGHT: What's love got to do with it? Well, Tina Turner looks happy enough to pose before the International Music Awards ceremony in 1993, but we don't think she actually owns a Harley.

demand." Are these the words of Richard Teerlink, the CEO behind the Harley-Davidson leveraged buy-out back in 1981? No, they express the philosophy behind the extraordinary success of Soichiro Honda. Nevertheless, despite that Japanese technological edge and chilling confidence, it took just five years from the buy-out for Harley-Davidson to wrest back the lead from Honda in the big bike home market; and the turnaround came against all the odds.

There's an old Japanese proverb: "To travel safely to Makurazaki in the south, look back over your shoulder to Wakkanai in the north and consider the pitfalls you have already encountered." There is no doubt that Harley-Davidson are followers of this dictum, not least because of the number of obstacles they have overcom in the course of their long history.

The transformation of a backyard hobby

RIGHT: Although exported all over the world, very few Harleys are seen in Red Square. A Russian militia man directs David Scott Barr, an American veteran riding round the world on his FLH.

RTL

ABOVE: **Chicago White Sox catcher Carlton Fisk gets what he always wanted on June 22, 1993 at Comiskey Park, to mark the all-time highest number of appearances behind the plate; this was his 2226th career game.**

RIGHT: **Two weeks to go in the presidential campaign, October 20, 1992. Gov. Bill Clinton knows just what to do in Milwaukee if you're on the campaign trail: get on a police spec Harley-Davidson and smile.**

into a company producing tens of thousands of machines in a few short years owed much to the happy accident of like-minded, talented brothers and friends being prepared to commit themsleves at the right time. The expansion of the Ford Motor Company in the 1920s, shortly followed by the Depression should have been enough to kill off any small motorcycle company, but the founders somehow continued to improve the product and market it successfully. The boom years of the Second World War were followed, almost inevitably, by decreased sales and increased competition. Once again the big twins pulled the company through the crisis and exports became even more vital and more vigorously pursued.

Economic strictures began to bite in more recent years and the 1981 management buy-out from AMF seemed sheer folly. The 13 H-D managers knew that the company had – and still has – a loyal customer base that most businesses only dream of. They had the managerial ability to introduce just-in-time inventory, so that desperately needed cash wasn't tied up in stock, and employee involvement, getting every member of the company committed to the product. By and large, complaints about Harley-Davidson build quality are a faded memory. From 1981 to 1991, productivity had doubled, market share was twice what it had been, and export revenue nearly trebled. It has to be admitted that this success is partly the result of borrowing working practices from the Japanese; but in terms of the machines themselves, that's about all that Harley-Davidson are borrowing from their competitors. Harley-Davidsons are still an intensely American icon – there's nothing like a Road King anywhere else in the huge motorcycle industry.

Enough facts and figures, they will never explain everything. You still see that old T-shirt around sometimes: "Harley-Davidson – If I Have to Explain, You Wouldn't Understand."

Attitude Is
Everything!

CHAPTER ELEVEN

STURGIS AND OTHER PARTIES

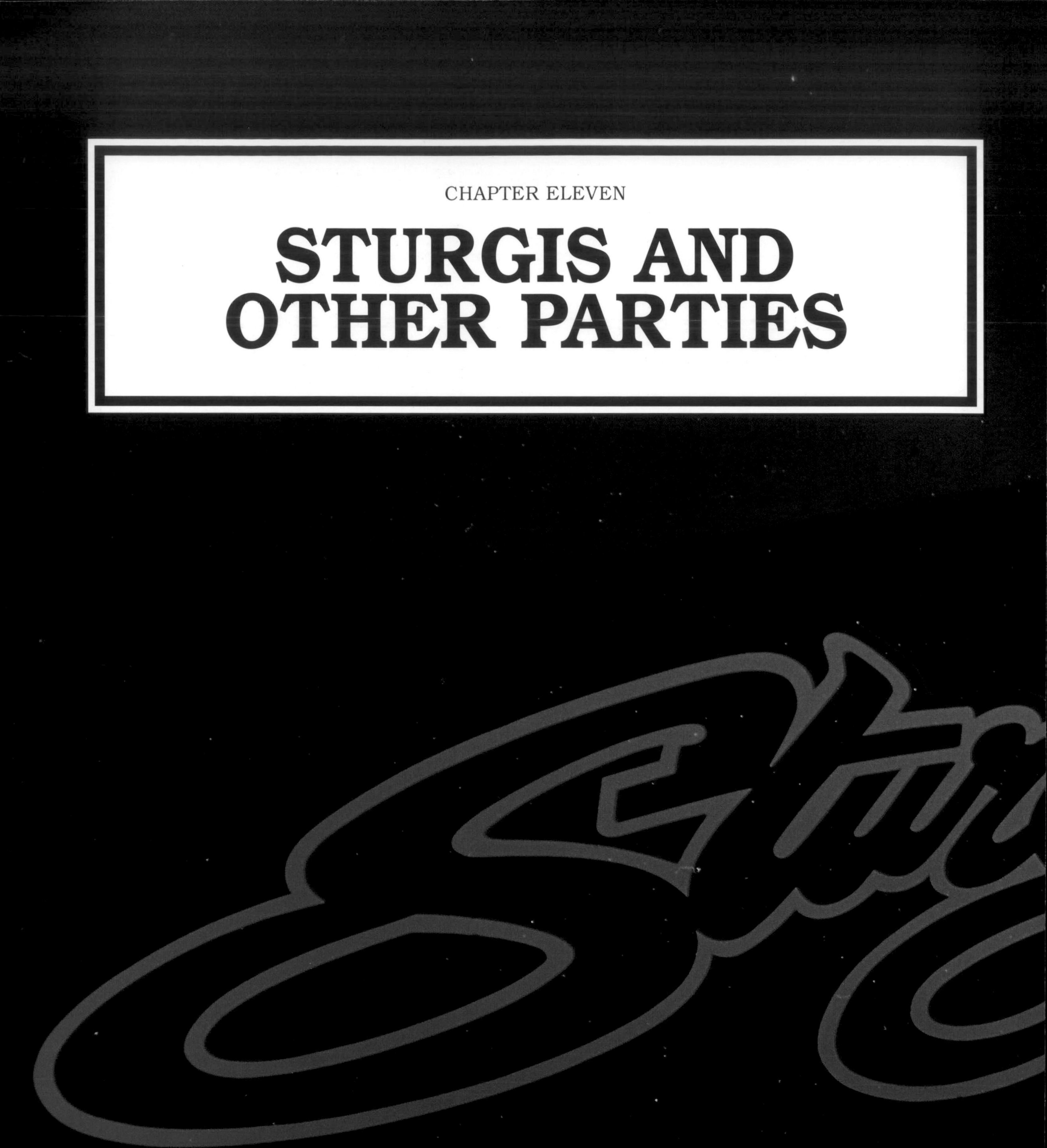

MOTOR
HARLEY-DAVIDSON
CYCLES

I asked a Sturgis veteran for his impressions of this, the most spectacular motorcycle gathering in the world. This is more or less the unexpurgated version from a rider who wished to remain anonymous. Then again, it might be a little poetic for some tastes, but each to his own.

"Catharsis time again. It's early August and my FLSTC Heritage Softail Classic is doing a steady 65 mph on Interstate 90. Destination? Sturgis, South Dakota, and the Black Hills Motorcycle Classic. The road is long but far from winding; mile after mile of laser-straight concrete induces a mental time out. A silly grin spreads across my face as I remember my first Harley, a '76 Sportster. The horn of a Peterbilt brings back the throb of the V-twin. Time to stop in Chamberlain for coffee and gas before crossing the Missouri river.

Pressing on past Presho, I admire the deep chrome of the forks as the highway glides by under the glistening blur of a barely undulating front wheel. Then I look around. The greenscape of South Dakota stretches from horizon to horizon, while above, white clouds placed as if by hand decorate a blue sky. I'm motorcycling in Cinemascope. After stopping at Wasta, I'm fed and watered and ready for a rapid final leg through Rapid City before leaving the Interstate at exit 32. I'm not alone. Hundreds of Harleys, together with Honda Gold Wings and Aspencades – Japan's two-wheeled Winnebagos – and a variety of BMW K100s and Kawasaki Ninjas, are streaming slowly down Junction Avenue to Main Street. If it's Monday, this must be Sturgis! Riding up one side of Main Street and down the other is a first gear ego trip that can last well into the night if you want it to; barricades manned by some mean-looking mothers ensure that motorcycles are the only vehicles allowed to enter. Naturally, Harleys predominate, but the Japanese 'big four' are strongly represented, Yamaha's Virago custom range being particularly popular. Classic British bikes, especially Triumphs ("Look, a Trident") always draw a crowd. And crowds there are, thousands of leather-clad figures spilling over from the sidewalks into the street. Amid V-twin music a galaxy of vendors aim to please, offering everything from Polish sausage to a ZZ top ticket, a tattoo to an oil change. Need a new chain for your '39 Knucklehead? Just ask. If you can't track down that elusive spare at Sturgis, give up. Main Street is simply, to use a well-worn phrase, Hog Heaven. There are wide boys riding Wide Glides; seriously fat boys riding Fat Boys; even small people on Low Rider Customs. As usual, trying to spot two Harleys exactly alike is virtually impossible – winning the state lottery would be easier. Want to personalize your bike while you're here? At the very least a friendly vendor will pinstripe your tank. The great and the not-so-good rev their iron on Main Street: airline pilots, doctors, teachers, dentists, product-liability

RIGHT: Main Street, Sturgis, South Dakota, 1992. The AMA-backed Black Hills rally began in 1938.

CITY OF STURGIS Welcomes You to STURGIS RALLY & RACES
SHOE REPAIR
Win this HARLEY-DAVIDSON
STOP
WELCOME
STURGIS

lawyers, truck drivers, cops (in and out of uniform), rock stars, insurance consultants, etcetera. If that isn't a priest on a '72 Electra Glide I'll eat my leather saddle bags. Harleys and Sturgis bring us together. After strutting your stuff it's time to park the bike and register at rally headquarters."

This annual ritual involves signing in and identifying your home town by sticking a pin on a map. There are already large clusters of pins around LA, Denver, Kansas City, Milwaukee (of course!), New York, St Louis, Wichita and Winnipeg. Most visitors have covered over 1000 miles; some, from as far as Miami, Florida, more than twice that distance. For many, devoting their annual vacation to Sturgis is the most natural thing in the world. Providing you've traveled to Sturgis as the rider or passenger of a motorcycle, you can enter a competition which includes the following categories:

1. Oldest rider attending the rally from the USA
2. Oldest rider attending the rally from Canada
3. Female rider coming the longest distance from Canada
4. Male rider coming the longest distance from Canada
5. Female rider coming the longest distance from the USA
6. Male rider coming the longest distance from the USA
7. Female rider coming the longest distance from a foreign country other than Canada
8. Male rider coming the longest distance from a foreign country other than Canada

The rally organizers present trophies to the winners.

Inside rally HQ you learn that the event dates back to 1938, when Sturgis resident and Indian motorcycle dealer J.C. 'Pappy' Hoel organized a two-day rally and race meeting under AMA sanction for the local Jackpine Gypsies motorcycle club, which he had formed two years earlier. Despite the sluggish recovery from the Great Depression, about 80 Black Hills folk from Deadwood, Lead and Rapid City managed the ride to the small farming town of Sturgis. On arrival, they camped in Pappy and Pearl's

If these pictures don't get your motor running, why are you reading this book? Every last Thursday in the month, HOG members congregate at the Hard Rock Café in West London. It's a stirring sight in the summer months, with up to 200 machines around, but it doesn't quite have the impact of Sturgis. Most of the machines in these photographs are post-Evo, but you can find plenty of old flatheads and knuckleheads taking a chance on the various organized tours.

Bob's
IOWA

backyard on Junction Avenue. Day one was spent exploring the grandeur of the Black Hills. On day two Sturgis Fairground's horse track reverberated to the thunder of engines at full bore as Indians and Harleys, sans lights and fenders, battled for victory. Few prisoners were taken and crashes were common. The spirit of that first meeting is still tangible today

The next task is to make camp. Finding accommodation at Sturgis is reassuringly easy. Campsites are plentiful, cheap and most come equipped with showers, toilets and laundry facilities. Many sites also provide food and live bands. Nightly blasts of rock 'n' roll (into the small hours) are for headbangers only and if you're past partying until sunrise, simply check with fellow campers before releasing the bungees. The Hog Campground five miles north of the drag strip on Hwy 79 offers welcome shade from 100-plus temperatures, as well as relative tranquility. It's H-D talk until well after dark: "See her coming off the Interstate? That Glide had more lights than the Brooklyn Bridge!" (or similar, less embarassingly self-conscious and corny comments).

Whether or not you're a member of the Harley Owners Group (HOG), or Ladies of Harley, a trip to the Harley-Davidson Traveling Show in Rapid City is a must. With 62 per cent of the domestic big bike market and the kind of brand loyalty other manufacturers would kill for, H-D hardly need the exposure, but customer care, as has been stressed earlier, is still a top priority. Inside Rushmore Plaza Center all of Harley's new models, branded accessories and leather clothing are on display. So is the gorgeous Ms Harley-Davidson; any young guns who fancy their chances had better have a motorcycle/sidecar combination, because her mom will want to come along too. Ladies of Harley have their own program, including a service seminar, a class at H-D's ride-in show, Scavenger Hunt and last, but by no means least, a Stud Your Duds Workshop.

At the HOG Hospitality Room, flash your membership card and get a free breakfast before being briefed about the Chapter Challenge and Observation Run. The merchandise area offers temptation beyond endurance, but most settle for a T-shirt. Outside in the sunshine there's the Harley-Davidson semi-trailer museum, a

Rushm
OFFICE
Bob's Family Restaur
Bob's
KODAK
FILM SOLD HERE
↓HERE↓
KODAK

RIGHT: The unmistakable face of Willie G., probably photographed at Sturgis more times than any machine.

ride-in bike show, field games, live music, a poker run – the whole enchilada. Sporting a black beret H-D's sage ambassador, Willie G., is easy to buttonhole and never too busy to talk with owners and enthusiasts. Paradoxically, having had your appetite well and truly whetted, demonstration rides are only available back in Sturgis, next to the Super 8 Motel at exit 30 off the Interstate. But people will ride all day for the chance to swing their legs over a new FLHTCU Tour Glide Ultra Classic, surely the king of motorcycles.

Set in the scenic Black Hills, Sturgis was (and is) the ideal location for a bike rally. The tours organized by rally HQ have always been hugely popular, attracting more riders year after year. One of the easiest is the Northern Hills Tour, snaking northwest into Wyoming along Interstate 90. Exit at Hwy 14 and it isn't long before the highlight of he tour looms into view – the Devils Tower, an exposed stack of volcanic rock standing 867 ft high, some 5117 ft above sea level. Devotees of director Stephen Spielberg will recognize it as the subject of Richard Dreyfuss's manic mudslinging in the motion picture *Close Encounters of the Third Kind.* Take the long way back to Sturgis by travell-

PREVIOUS PAGES: Electra Glides, Wide Glides, Sportsters – now what's that creme and brown object disappearing to the left, with the whitewall tire? Genuine fabulous fifties, or just a nostalgic paint scheme?

RIGHT: A little more Eagle Iron silver on the bike, and as the years pass, a little more chrome in the beard, but the passion never dies.

ing north on Hwy 24 to Hulett before turning east en route for Aladdin, Wyoming, where the wise buy a cooling sarsaparilla from the town's charming general store, which seems pleasantly stuck in the 1890s.

The similarities between riding a Harley and being a cowboy in the Old West are too obvious to ignore in these kinds of surroundings. You sit in a saddle and the saddlebags wouldn't look out of place slung across the back of a mustang. You're riding with the spirit of cowpunches and gunslingers who were proud of their freedom and independence. Sturgis gives riders the opportunity to head out into the Black Hills and live the dream by being part of the Old West.

'Calamity Jane' wasn't invented by Hollywood, she really existed. 'Calamity' (real name Martha Jane) lived in Deadwood Gulch, a gold rush town that sprang up overnight. Doris Day's song immortalized her: "Oh the Deadwood Stage is comin' on over the hill, where Indian arrows are thicker than porcupine quills." Since Calamity's time the name of the town has been shortened to Deadwood, but little else appears to have changed. Some of the

buildings are over a century old and you half expect James Butler ('Wild Bill') Hickok to walk into the saloon at any moment. In the Belle Union Theatre Jack McCall was acquitted of Hickok's murder, only to the tried a second time and hanged in Yankton, South Dakota nine months later. Cowboys didn't have to worry about parking, but today anyone who disregards thc 'No Parking' signs in the center of Deadwood will collect a $100 fine.

Sturgis is also the perfect jumping-off point for tours to Old Fort Meade (not far from where General George A. Custer camped his fateful 1874 expedition), taking in the Custer Monument and Bear Butte; the Southern Hills Ride; the Eastern Ride (including the awesome B-1 strategic bombers of Ellsworth AFB, as well as Wall Drug and the Badlands); and perhaps everyone's favorite, the Mount Rushmore Ride. Any photographer will tell you that the best time to capture Rushmore's four presidents is early in the morning, when the sun shines directly on the rock.

Racing is as much a part of Sturgis as touring. The Black Hills Speedway in Rapid City and Sturgis Fairgrounds holds AMA national and regional half-mile dirt track events for vintage (that means built before 1975) machines. The Jackpine Gypsies Club Grounds host short track events and a vintage Tourist Trophy (TT) meeting. Unless you take the precaution of being upwind in the action, the hill climbs will be all but obscured by dust. Friday night is when the leading AMA professional riders descend on Club Grounds for the big 600 short track national shootout. (The Honda RS750 brought to an end the supremacy of the H-D XR750 on the dirt track from the mid-1980s.) Junior riders are mounted on Rotax-powered 600 cc single-cylinder Woods and Harley-Davidson machines. The biggest draw by far are the Harley-only drag races; the Sturgis Dragway makes time for street bike one-on-ones, as well as the professional nitro action.Towards the end of rally week the faithful gather at the Rat's Hole Custom Bike Show organized by Karl ('Big Daddy Rat') Smith. A regular attraction at Daytona until 1987, this event features the best in custom craftsmanship.

At the end of the 1970s Willie G. rolled up

BELOW: California, Connecticut, and Mount Rushmore; one nation under God. The Mount Rushmore ride out of Sturgis is very popular.

RIGHT: Unmistakable front profile, maybe heading back to town to take a look at the short track 600 races on Friday night.

ABOVE: **Egg pickup at the Am Jam, New York State, 1991. It isn't only Sturgis and Daytona that get all the fun of course.**

TOP: **The dragsters are always one of the most popular sights at Sturgis.**

on a belt-drive Lowrider, to general approval from the assembled masses. Apart from the fun of flying the company flag and giving riders a sense of being part of the ongoing H-D saga, meetings like Sturgis can be an effective way of taking a mighty big straw poll on a new design. It isn't only Sturgis of course. There are unofficial meetings, some at dealerships, some at eateries or bars across the States. I once saw two Sportsters outside a very expensive restaurant in Jokkmokk, Sweden on the Arctic Circle. Does that count as a meeting?

The third European HOG rally was held in 1993 at the slightly warmer Bosbadhoeven in Holland. Flatheads, knuckleheads, panheads, even servicars could be admired amongst the younger machinery, some of it ridden by GIs stationed in Europe; and once again, Willie G. was on hand to make them feel a little less homesick, alongside Vice President Clyde Fessler. Willie G.'s son Bill was there as well. A 1500-bike ride-out, a fashion show, an auction for Harley-Davidson's favored charity, the Muscular Dystrophy appeal, a massive beer tent, a swimming pool, what more could one ask?

Back home, Daytona Bike Week rivals Sturgis as the greatest H-D gathering. Nobody seems to have done a proper head count in the March Florida sunshine, but 250,000 would seem to be the average guess. Swap meets, the H-D show at the Hilton, test-rides, the racing of course, some events sanctioned by the company and some most definitely not, make it an extraordinary celebration. The fact that it's not specifically about Harley-Davidson machinery seems to be lost on most.

One more example; you could go on listing H-D meets across the globe for ever, but they're all essentially about one thing. Admiring individual machines and individuated machines, while confirming the common thread binding the participants – we belong to Milwaukee, we've never been west of Munich or London, and our machines have been emasculated by European laws – but we don't care. On August Bank Holiday Monday every year, the HDRCGB (Rider's Club of Great Britain) organizes the Shipley Rally. 500-odd – some really quite odd – machines ride in convoy to a steam rally. Small beer in comparison with Sturgis? Well yes, but multiply the event and set it down in Sweden or France or Germany, and it looks a little more important for export orders. And notice the huge amount of interest generated along the route of the ride, people waiting patiently to listen for the thunder to pass.

RIGHT: **A parade for Harley-Davidson's 90th anniversary from the state fairgrounds to the lake front, Milwaukee. More than 25,000 were estimated to have taken part.**

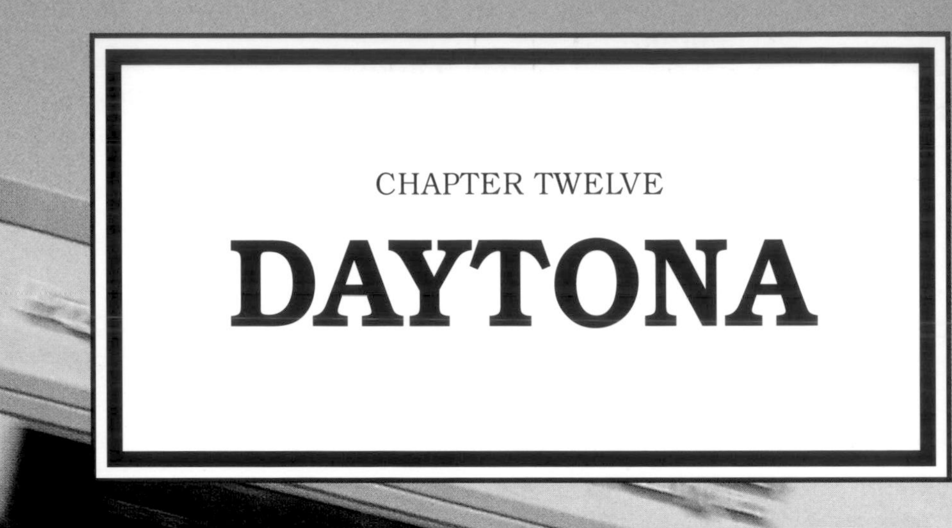

CHAPTER TWELVE

DAYTONA

Some of the Daytona story is told elsewhere in this book, but the close association of Harley-Davidson with the venue is worth looking at in a little more detail, not least to see the ups and downs of H-D fortunes and compare them with parallel successes and failures in the production bike market.

In 1975 Jim Dunn managed to take his Harley-Davidson to 17th position at the Daytona International Speedway. It was no mean feat in a year when Yamaha took 18 of the top 20 places, building on the kind of domination that has seen them win virtually every Daytona 200 between 1972 and the present day. Back in '75 Harley-Davidson were to take their last top 20 position in the event, after over 30 seasons of prevailing over some of the best bikes in the world, winning the Daytona 200 16 times in the process.

America's main motorcycle race has its roots in the post-Depression revival of motorcycling in the United States. Before the 1930s the sport had been in decline due to the manufacturers' insistence on limiting the horsepower of racing models after a series of serious injuries and deaths. Part and parcel of H-D's continuing battle, often fought through the AMA, was to keep the image of motorcycling acceptable to non-riders. With the Depression, America entered its worst period of economic history and motorcycle racing, along with everything else, suffered from the lack of finance. Manufacturers had to cut back on production while fans had little to spend on visiting meets.

1932 saw an attempt to stop the decline when a group of enthusiasts resurrected a long-distance racing event that had run in the 1920s in Savannah, Georgia. The first 200 mile race was won by a Harley-Davidson ridden by Ralph Edwards. The race, dominated by Harley-Davidson, ran at Savannah and Jacksonville, Florida for the next five years until another city in Florida persuaded the race organizers to use their beach, previously a speed run, for the 1937 race. The city was Daytona Beach and the Daytona 200 had begun.

That first race saw the riders take on the newly-built 3.2 mile course running the length of the beach and the nearby highway. The two 1.2 mile straights were joined by sandy turns. Indian were to take the honors, with Harley-Davidson coming third, fifth, sixth and tenth. As the meager Depression years faded, 15,000 race fans turned out.

Harley-Davidson would have to wait until the following year to stamp their mark on the event. Ben Campanale broke the 200 mile record in a time of two hours 42 minutes, while the Harleys of Tom Hayes and Griffin Kathcart roared into the third and fourth spots. Campanale was to become the first two-time winner by triumphing in the 1939 event, breaking his own record by six minutes in the process. An outstanding start to the new event was completed in

PREVIOUS PAGES: **Leading the parade to Harley Heaven at Daytona, 1993.**

RIGHT: **What used to be called a Full Dresser rolls into town for Daytona bike week.**

DAYTONA BEACH
WELCOMES BIKERS
BIKE WEEK '92
MOTOR
HARLEY-DAVIDSON
CYCLES
Welcome
Welcome
We're Glad
You're Here!
Peninsula
JIFFY
FOOD
STORE
WALK

ABOVE: **Daytona Beach was, of course, a record-breaking venue as well as a race track. "Flying cop" H. A. Patterson chased Indian racer Johnny Seymour's 1926 world mile record. Seymour took the record again in 1932, and lost it after a long period of Indian possession of the straight mile speed, to Joe Petrali on a modified 61E, in 1936.**

1940 when Babe Tancred took his Harley-Davidson WLDR first to the flag. For Campanale there was intense disappointment; breaking down halfway through the race, his dream of three consecutive victories and the permanent ownership of the race trophy disappeared. There followed a lean period for the Harleys. In 1941, Billy Matthews' Norton came in first, leaving Harley-Davidson all the other top ten positions. The H-D tactic of packing the races to gain a result didn't quite come off that time. In 1947 (the race was cancelled during the war years) they still dominated the event, with 14 of the top placings, but failing to take the top two positions. It would not be until 1953 that Harley-Davidson would take the cup with Paul Goldsmith, but that event was to usher in a period of Harley supremacy easily surpassing their early domination of the event.

The comeback was in part due to the introduction of the 45 cu.in. KR. The old WR had proved itself outdated and the new engine was like a breath of fresh, higher

ABOVE: Vintage Sixty One racer at Daytona Speedway. It wasn't until 1914 that H-D set up its first official racing department.

LEFT: Close racing for the 883s at Daytona, 1993.

ABOVE: The XR-750 performed with honor on the dirt for many years, but it would be Yamaha who would take up the mantle. The old iron barrel XR-750 had straight silver exhausts, the aluminum-engined model had flat black megaphones up high.

compression air to the riders. Harley-Davidson were not to get it all their own way in the ensuing years. While Indian had announced that they could no longer finance a race team, BSA emerged as Harley-Davidson's great rivals, if on a somewhat irregular basis. While they managed to take the top five positions in 1954, BSA could only manage seventh in 1955, trailing Triumph and Norton and Harley-Davidsons in first, second and third.

1955 would see a run of victories begin for Harley-Davidson that would only be beaten by Yamaha in the 1970s and early 1980s. They were victorious seven times in a row, taking five of the next eight cups as well. The tussle with BSA would continue in 1956 and 1957 but it was the races of the next three years where Harley-Davidson exercised true dominance.

Joe Leonard was the defending champion in 1958. He set the fastest qualifying speed and in the race itself his 200 mile record of 99.68 mph would remain unbeatable on the beach course. Harleys took the top seven slots and a total of 13 out of the top 20, the sort of whitewash that Harley-Davidson had last achieved in the early 1940s. Much the same happened in 1959 with Brad Andres finishing first, Dick Mann second, Tony Murquia third, Jack Gholson fourth and Bobby Sirkegian fifth. Brad Andres became only the fourth rider to win back to back in 1960 in what was a truly astonishing result for Harley-Davidson. In what was to be the last race run on the beach course, Brad Andres had to fight tooth and nail over the first half of the course with the lead changing 12 times between Carroll Resweber, Roger Reiman and Andres himself. Only when his opponents had to drop into the pits could Andres feel secure, unheaded to the finish. While Andres' victory was spectacular, the performance of the Harleys overall was outstanding, the bikes taking the top 14 spots, the first time a make had taken the first ten places, and then some!

In 1961 the race moved to the Daytona International Speedway track. The beach course had become unfeasible as a venue, in the main due to the deterioration of the course. The construction of the track had been planned since 1953 by Bill France Sr. and in action since 1959 running NASCAR stock car races, and the move had been on the cards since then. It was not without its difficulties, however, with concerns voiced about the race taking place on banked turns. These were soon resolved and the first race on the new course, in 1961, was run of a flat two mile course within the circuit. Despite the new course and conditions Harley-Davidsons still dominated, with

LEFT: AMA victor Chris Carr at Daytona in 1993.

BELOW: Aermacchi single-cylinder vintage racer at Daytona.

DAYTONA BEACH
WELCOMES BIKERS
Harley Davidson

PREVIOUS PAGES: **Daytona never stops, night or day. It is not a Harley-Davidson event of course, but you can't see many of the new Triumphs in this picture.**

RIGHT: **Sportsters and others on the beach. The company will let you have a test ride of the latest models if you show your license and you look as if they can trust you with the precious merchandise.**

KAY'S
Fine Dining...
at Modest Prices
2 BLOCKS WEST ON MAIN STREET
DOMINO
25
DAY

RIGHT: A little discreet advertising at the show grounds.

Roger Reiman in first place and a sprinkling of H-Ds in the top 20. The ominous second place of Don Burnett's Triumph was to set the scene for the next six races as the two makes battled it out for supremacy.

Any fears Harley-Davidson may have had were well founded the following year when Don Burnett and his Triumph took the checkered flag followed the Matchless of Dick Mann. While Harleys took the next three places, it was a rude awakening following their virtual domination of the race. They came back the following year to begin yet another run of three consecutive victories through Ralph White and Roger Reiman (twice). Both Harley-Davidson and Triumph were reaching the end of their glory days as the 1960s drew to a close. Triumph won in 1966 and 1967, while Harley-Davidson took the flag in 1968 and 1969, their last victory to date in the event.

Why did the glory days have to end for Harley-Davidson? The Japanese, of course, came on the scene. 1968 saw Yamaha and Suzuki enter the event for the first time, Yamaha promptly taking the second and third places and Suzuki fifth. 1969 saw the arrival of Kawasaki and 1970 Honda, who, with Dick Mann at the helm, became the first Japanese motorbike manufacturers to win the event. Harley-Davidson could only manage sixth, 15th and 18th, and in truth, the writing was on the wall. They only managed six top 20 places in the next five years, succumbing to an almost total Japanese dominance that has few American or European bikes getting a look-in in the 20 years or so since 1973.

ABOVE: Another one you won't find in the official Harley-Davidson catalog.

LEFT: Somewhere in there is a 1990 Springer Softail, at the Rat's Hole custom show, Daytona 1993.

ABOVE: The most interesting thing about this photograph is, of course, the full valanced fenders . . .

LEFT: Another custom machine at Daytona Beach, with neat bikini fairing and equally neat hat. A distinctive FXLR Low Rider Custom.

RIGHT: Every man's American dream? A babe, a bike and a beach.

MOTOR

RIGHT: Beautiful Screamin' Eagle pipes; viewed up close like this, they're a true sculpture for the machine age.

TERMINATOR

LEFT: A popular and highly skilled competition on the beach.

RIGHT: The Great American Rodeo at Daytona. Note the bulky Tour Glide fairing, but not factory paint scheme.

RIGHT: A line-up of vintage machinery at the Great American Rodeo.

RODEO Sweetheart

THE
Black Dahlia
II

LEFT: Fabulous custom job at the Rat's Hole custom show.

RIGHT: The death's head features on many tanks, but this one between the jugs is particularly effective.

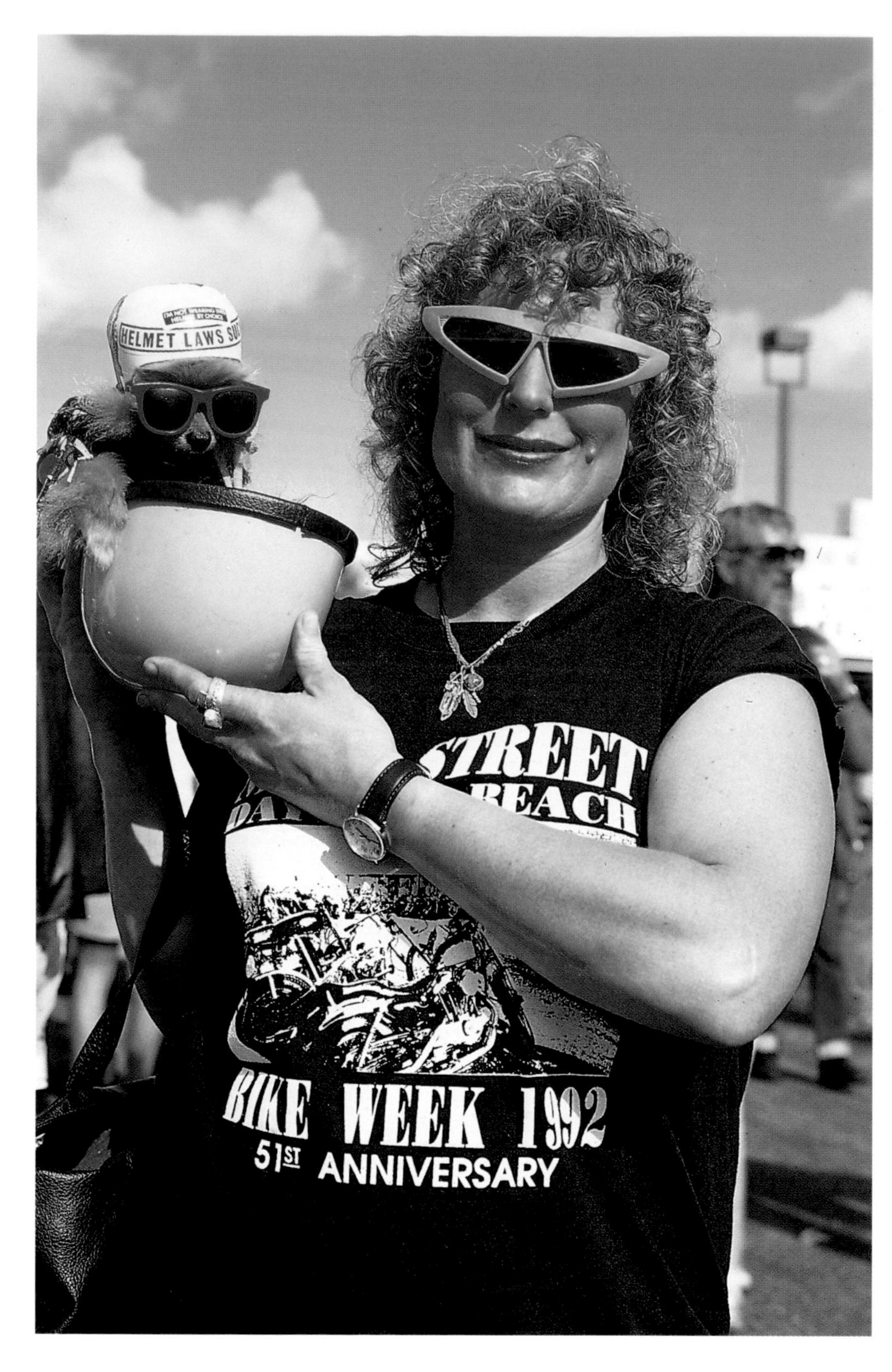

ABOVE: Making a point about helmet laws at one of the biggest motorcycle parties in the world.

RIGHT: How much more can you do to a machine? It doesn't look like a V-twin. From the headlight cowl to the air cleaner cover, none of it looks standard, and it's difficult to tell if any of it is even "official" H-D bolt-ons. In fact, is it a Harley at all?

1937 Beach/Road Course

FINISH	MAKE
1st	Indian
2nd	Norton
3rd	**Harley-Davidson**
4th	Indian
5th	**Harley-Davidson**
6th	**Harley-Davidson**
7th	Indian
8th	Indian
9th	Indian
10th	**Harley-Davidson**

1938 Beach/Road Course

FINISH	MAKE
1st	**Harley-Davidson**
2nd	Indian
3rd	**Harley-Davidson**
4th	**Harley-Davidson**
5th	Indian
6th	**Harley-Davidson**
7th	**Harley-Davidson**
8th	**Harley-Davidson**
9th	Indian
10th	Ariel

1939 Beach/Road Course

FINISH	MAKE
1st	**Harley-Davidson**
2nd	**Harley-Davidson**
3rd	Indian
4th	Vincent
5th	**Harley-Davidson**
6th	**Harley-Davidson**
7th	**Harley-Davidson**
8th	**Harley-Davidson**
9th	**Harley-Davidson**
10th	**Harley-Davidson**

1940 Beach/Road Course

FINISH	MAKE
1st	**Harley-Davidson**
2nd	Indian
3rd	**Harley-Davidson**
4th	**Harley-Davidson**
5th	**Harley-Davidson**
6th	**Harley-Davidson**
7th	**Harley-Davidson**
8th	Indian
9th	**Harley-Davidson**
10th	**Harley-Davidson**

1941 Beach/Road Course

FINISH	MAKE
1st	Norton
2nd	**Harley-Davidson**
3rd	**Harley-Davidson**
4th	**Harley-Davidson**
5th	**Harley-Davidson**
6th	**Harley-Davidson**
7th	**Harley-Davidson**
8th	**Harley-Davidson**
9th	**Harley-Davidson**
10th	**Harley-Davidson**

1947 Beach/Road Course

FINISH	MAKE
1st	Indian
2nd	Indian
3rd	**Harley-Davidson**
4th	**Harley-Davidson**
5th	**Harley-Davidson**
6th	**Harley-Davidson**
7th	**Harley-Davidson**
8th	Triumph
9th	**Harley-Davidson**
10th	**Harley-Davidson**

1948 Beach/Road Course

FINISH	MAKE
1st	Indian
2nd	Norton
3rd	**Harley-Davidson**
4th	Indian
5th	**Harley-Davidson**
6th	Triumph
7th	**Harley-Davidson**
8th	**Harley-Davidson**
9th	**Harley-Davidson**
10th	BMW

1949 Beach/Road Course

FINISH	MAKE
1st	Norton
2nd	Norton
3rd	Norton
4th	**Harley-Davidson**
5th	**Harley-Davidson**
6th	BSA
7th	Indian
8th	**Harley-Davidson**
9th	**Harley-Davidson**
10th	**Harley-Davidson**

1950 Beach/Road Course

FINISH	MAKE
1st	Norton
2nd	Norton
3rd	BSA
4th	Norton
5th	**Harley-Davidson**
6th	**Harley-Davidson**
7th	Norton
8th	**Harley-Davidson**
9th	**Harley-Davidson**
10th	**Harley-Davidson**

1951 Beach/Road Course

FINISH	MAKE
1st	Norton
2nd	Norton
3rd	Triumph
4th	Triumph
5th	Norton
6th	Triumph
7th	BSA
8th	**Harley-Davidson**
9th	Triumph
10th	**Harley-Davidson**

1952 Beach/Road Course

FINISH	MAKE
1st	Norton
2nd	Norton
3rd	Triumph
4th	Norton
5th	BSA
6th	Norton
7th	Norton
8th	Triumph
9th	BSA
10th	BSA

(Harley-Davidson 15th, 17th & 18th)

1953 Beach/Road Course

FINISH	MAKE
1st	**Harley-Davidson**
2nd	Triumph
3rd	Norton
4th	Norton
5th	BSA
6th	Triumph
7th	**Harley-Davidson**
8th	BSA
9th	BSA
10th	**Harley-Davidson**

1954 Beach/Road Course

FINISH	MAKE
1st	BSA
2nd	BSA
3rd	BSA
4th	BSA
5th	BSA
6th	Triumph
7th	Triumph
8th	BSA
9th	Triumph
10th	**Harley-Davidson**

1955 Beach/Road Course

FINISH	MAKE
1st	**Harley-Davidson**
2nd	**Harley-Davidson**
3rd	**Harley-Davidson**
4th	Triumph
5th	Norton
6th	Triumph
7th	BSA
8th	**Harley-Davidson**
9th	BSA
10th	**Harley-Davidson**

1956 Beach/Road Course

FINISH	MAKE
1st	**Harley-Davidson**
2nd	BSA
3rd	BSA
4th	BSA
5th	BSA
6th	**Harley-Davidson**
7th	**Harley-Davidson**
8th	**Harley-Davidson**
9th	**Harley-Davidson**
10th	**Harley-Davidson**

1957 Beach/Road Course

FINISH	MAKE
1st	**Harley-Davidson**
2nd	BSA
3rd	BSA
4th	Triumph
5th	BSA
6th	**Harley-Davidson**
7th	**Harley-Davidson**
8th	BSA
9th	BSA
10th	BSA

1958 Beach/Road Course

FINISH	MAKE
1st	**Harley-Davidson**
2nd	**Harley-Davidson**
3rd	**Harley-Davidson**
4th	**Harley-Davidson**
5th	**Harley-Davidson**
6th	**Harley-Davidson**
7th	**Harley-Davidson**
8th	**Triumph**
9th	BSA
10th	**Harley-Davidson**

1959 Beach/Road Course

FINISH	MAKE
1st	**Harley-Davidson**
2nd	**Harley-Davidson**
3rd	**Harley-Davidson**
4th	**Harley-Davidson**
5th	**Harley-Davidson**
6th	Triumph
7th	BSA
8th	**Harley-Davidson**
9th	BSA
10th	**Harley-Davidson**

1960 Beach/Road Course

FINISH	MAKE
1st	**Harley-Davidson**
2nd	**Harley-Davidson**
3rd	**Harley-Davidson**
4th	**Harley-Davidson**
5th	**Harley-Davidson**
6th	**Harley-Davidson**
7th	**Harley-Davidson**
8th	**Harley-Davidson**
9th	**Harley-Davidson**
10th	**Harley-Davidson**

1961 Speedway Course

FINISH	MAKE
1st	**Harley-Davidson**
2nd	Triumph
3rd	**Harley-Davidson**
4th	BSA
5th	**Harley-Davidson**
6th	Triumph
7th	**Harley-Davidson**
8th	BSA
9th	**Harley-Davidson**
10th	**Harley-Davidson**

1962 Speedway Course

FINISH	MAKE
1st	Triumph
2nd	Matchless
3rd	**Harley-Davidson**
4th	**Harley-Davidson**
5th	**Harley-Davidson**
6th	BSA
7th	BSA
8th	BSA
9th	**Harley-Davidson**
10th	**Harley-Davidson**

1963 Speedway Course

FINISH	MAKE
1st	**Harley-Davidson**
2nd	Triumph
3rd	**Harley-Davidson**
4th	**Harley-Davidson**
5th	BSA
6th	BSA
7th	**Harley-Davidson**
8th	BSA
9th	**Harley-Davidson**
10th	**Harley-Davidson**

1964 Speedway Course

FINISH	MAKE
1st	**Harley-Davidson**
2nd	Triumph
3rd	**Harley-Davidson**
4th	**Harley-Davidson**
5th	Matchless
6th	Matchless
7th	BSA
8th	Norton
9th	**Harley-Davidson**
10th	BSA

1965 Speedway Course

FINISH	MAKE
1st	**Harley-Davidson**
2nd	**Harley-Davidson**
3rd	**Triumph**
4th	Triumph
5th	Matchless
6th	Triumph
7th	**Harley-Davidson**
8th	BSA
9th	**Harley-Davidson**
10th	**Harley-Davidson**

1966 Speedway Course

FINISH	MAKE
1st	Triumph
2nd	**Harley-Davidson**
3rd	**Harley-Davidson**
4th	Matchless
5th	**Harley-Davidson**
6th	Triumph
7th	**Harley-Davidson**
8th	**Harley-Davidson**
9th	Triumph
10th	**Harley-Davidson**

1967 Speedway Course

FINISH	MAKE
1st	Triumph
2nd	Triumph
3rd	**Harley-Davidson**
4th	**Harley-Davidson**
5th	**Harley-Davidson**
6th	**Harley-Davidson**
7th	Triumph
8th	Triumph
9th	Triumph
10th	Triumph

1968 Speedway Course

FINISH	MAKE
1st	**Harley-Davidson**
2nd	Yamaha
3rd	Yamaha
4th	**Harley-Davidson**
5th	Suzuki
6th	Triumph
7th	Triumph
8th	Matchless
9th	Suzuki
10th	Honda

1969 Speedway Course

FINISH	MAKE
1st	**Harley-Davidson**
2nd	Suzuki
3rd	Yamaha
4th	**Harley-Davidson**
5th	Yamaha
6th	**Harley-Davidson**
7th	Yamaha
8th	Yamaha
9th	Triumph
10th	**Harley-Davidson**

1970 Speedway Course

FINISH	MAKE
1st	Honda
2nd	Triumph
3rd	Triumph
4th	Yamaha
5th	Suzuki
6th	**Harley-Davidson**
7th	Kawasaki
8th	Triumph
9th	Kawasaki
10th	Yamaha

1971 Speedway Course

FINISH	MAKE
1st	BSA
2nd	Triumph
3rd	BSA
4th	**Harley-Davidson**
5th	Yamaha
6th	Yamaha
7th	Triumph
8th	Triumph
9th	Kawasaki
10th	Yamaha

Harley-Davidson achieved their last top ten position in this race with Roger Reiman. Their last top 20 place came four years later.

BELOW: Roger Reiman on an XR-750, Daytona, March 1967.

INDEX

ACKNOWLEDGMENTS

The author and publisher would like to thank the following for their help in the preparation of this book: Design-23, Sara Dunphy for the picture research, Helen Dawson for the index and Judith Millidge, the editor. The author is particularly grateful to Mick Walker for his contribution to the racing chapter. The following individuals and institutions have granted permission for use of the pictures on the pages noted below.

The Bettmann Archive: 39, 66-67, 136 (top), 138

BFI: 201

Malcolm Birkitt: 6-7, 9, 12, 17, 20 (below R), 34-35, 44-45, 149, 154-5, 161 (top), 164-165, 175 (top), 176 (top), 180, 188

BPL: 65 (below), 103

Brooklands Museum: 135 (top)

Kel Edge: 230-231

EMAP: 31 (below), 38-39, 101 (below)

Jeff Hackett: 4-5, 13, 14-15, 18, 20 (below L), 28, 31, 40-41, 42, 60-61, 65 (top), 68, 82-83, 85, 86-87, 87 (top), 88 (below), 90-91, 93, 95, 96, 97, 98-99, 100, 103, 106, 107 (top), 112-113, 116-117, 124-125, 126-127, 128, 129, 140 (top), 141, 147, 148, 150 (below), 151, 152 (top), 153, 159 (top), 160-161, 166, 172-173, 174, 175 (bottom), 177, 178 (all 4), 179, 181 (both), 182, 183, 184, 189, 190-191, 194, 215, 220, 224 (both), 225, 226-227, 231 (top), 233 (both), 238, 239 (below), 242-243, 245 (top), 248, 249

IWM: 47 (top), 50-51 (all 3), 54, 55 (both), 59 (top), 57 (both), 58, 59 (both)

Mac McDiarmid: 1, 2-3, 150, 175 (top), 186-187, 196, 212-213

Andrew Morland: 32, 37, 48, 52-53, 56 (below), 63, 70, 72-73, 76-77, 104-105, 110-111, 115, 119 (top), 122 (top), 144, 246

National Film Archive: 200

National Motor Museum, Beaulieu: 29, 134

Garry Stuart: 10-11 (both), 16, 19 (both), 20 (top), 21, 25, 26, 43 (both), 49, 69, 75, 78-79 (top), 80 (below), 94, 101 (top), 108-109, 120, 152 (middle), 157, 167, 168-169, 176 (below), 185 (both), 193, 195 (top), 199, 216, 217 (both), 222, 223, 229, 234-235, 236-237, 239 (top), 240 (top), 241, 244, 245 (below), 247

UPI/Bettmann: 22-23, 27, 130-131, 197 (below), 208-209, 210, 211

Mick Walker: 33, 47 (below), 58, 76 (below), 77, 78-79 (below), 80 (top), 84, 88 (top), 94, 102, 118 (both), 121, 123, 142, 143, 145, 158, 159 (below), 162, 163, 253